Vegan Slow Cooker Cookbook

100 Tasty Vegan Slow Cooker Recipes For Life Long Health

By Jessica Brooks

are for clarifying purposes only and are the owned by the owners themselves, not affiliated with this document.

Disclaimer – Please read!

The information provided in this book is designed to provide helpful information on the subjects discussed. This book is not meant to be used, nor should it be used, to diagnose or treat any medical condition. For diagnosis or treatment of any medical problem, consult your own physician. The publisher and author are not responsible for any specific health or allergy needs that may require medical supervision and are not liable for any damages or negative consequences from any treatment, action, application or preparation, to any person reading or following the information in this book. References are provided for informational purposes only and do not constitute endorsement of any websites or other sources. Readers should be aware that the websites listed in this book may change.

Table Of Contents

Main dishes

Desserts to end your feast

Free Ebook Offer..**123**

Free Preview Of "The Vegan Diet For Beginners" **124**
About the Author **132**
Valerian Press..**133**

Introduction

I am happy to present you a healthy cookbook with some of the best vegan slow cooker recipes that you can cook with ease and convenience. If you are a busy mom, then this book is for you to have your nutritious meal ready, even if you do not get the time to monitor the cooking. Moreover, all the recipes are vegan, so you do not have to worry if you are following a 'no dairy, no animal product' diet. Veganism is a healthy option too!

A slow cooker keeps the nutrition of the food intact while, letting all the ingredients cook at a low temperature with no burning at all. The recipes given in this book will suit taste patterns for all. For instance, if your kid is choosy about food, then you can prepare some kids-friendly recipes given here to set your little one's mood. Also, I have included recipes that you can dish up for your guests at any occasion. Not only for your guests, but you can indulge in a lavish cooking spree with your recipes to please your family as well.

I have categorized the top 100 vegan slow cooking recipes as breakfast recipes, main-dish recipes, snack/appetizer recipes, soup recipes and dessert recipes to make things easier for you to find. Also, I have used all vegan substitutes in place of animal products and dairy products. This book will definitely make you a vegan cooking pro!

Benefits of Vegan Food

These days we get to see many people turning vegetarian due to health as well as ethical reasons, and those who take vegetarianism a step further are called vegans. Vegans can be called a 'strict vegetarian' who abstains from consuming all animal products. Animal products that vegans do not eat include meat, chicken, eggs and fish. Dairy products along with honey, come under animal-by products, hence vegans do not include them in their diet either.

The main motive behind veganism is 'man should not exploit animals'. This doctrine was coined by Donald Watson in 1944, who later established the Vegan Society in England. Till 2000, veganism was an isolated term, but restaurants and supermarkets have popularized vegan food so much that veganism has turned into a healthy and popular diet alternative.

Health is not the only reason, ethical and environmental reasons also led many people to follow veganism. Some vegans even refrain from using things made of animal skins and other animal by-products, in their day to day life. This is called ethical veganism, whereas environmental veganism refers to averting animal farming. Vegans depend on a plant-based diet that is loaded with green veggies, nuts, soy, legumes and grains. Fruits are also largely included to make food delicious as well as healthy.

Whatever diet you choose, it is essential to be rich in all the nutrients required by a human body. In a vegan diet, proteins are added by using soy, chickpeas, lentils, kale, whole wheat, potato, broccoli, peas, etc. Vegan foods usually contain less calories and saturated fats. Seed butter, nut butter, nuts, avocado, coconut, margarine and oil are the major sources of fat in vegan diet. Vitamin D is obtained from rice milk and soy milk. Iron, calcium, zinc are added to vegan food by including raisins, orange juice, prune juice, dark green leafy veggies, millet, kale etc.

There may be some challenges following a vegan diet, especially if you are pregnant and have kids in the family because keeping a check on nutrition is highly important for babies and pregnant ladies. In such cases, you must follow a diet that is healthy for them and contains healthy ingredients reminiscent to animal proteins.

All animal products are substituted by vegan ingredients in this book, so you will not have any issue while cooking. Enjoy slow cooking with vegan recipes!

Breakfast Recipes

Breakfast is the most essential part of a diet because it gives us energy for the whole day. Whatever food we eat in breakfast should be healthy and loaded with almost all essential nutrients in order to have vitality and vigor for the entire day. Moreover, in the morning we feel hungry due to a long gap between last nights dinner and breakfast the next morning, so we should try and eat only nutritious meals to cope with the nourishing requirement of your body. So, gear up, get ready with your kitchen tools and slow cooker to make some hearty breakfast dishes.

Note: All breakfast recipes in this section are vegan and I have taken care to not use any ingredient that may harm your sentiments for animals. Also, these are slow cooker recipes, so you can put your ingredients a night before in a slow cooker to enjoy the dish in the morning.

Vegan S'mores marshmallows oatmeal

Good news that vegan marshmallows are available now! So, get them and whip up this great breakfast dish.

Serves: 2-3

Ingredients:
- Steel-cut oats – ½ cup
- Unsweetened coconut milk- 2 cups
- Vanilla extract – 1 teaspoon

For S'mores
- Vegan chocolate chips and Graham crackers – ¼ cup each, finely chopped
- Vegan marshmallows – ¼ cup

Method
At night: grease your 1-1 ½ slow cooker and fill with milk, oats and vanilla. Cook on low for the whole night.

In the morning: Stir the content well to avoid watery consistency. Add all the S'mores topping contents and let the marshmallows and chocolate melt. Enjoy!

Coconut lemon pancake

With flavorful coconut milk and healthy flaxseed with whole wheat flour, these pancakes will surely woo your taste buds!

Serves: 15

Ingredients:
Dry:
- Whole wheat pastry flour – 1 cup
- Shredded coconut – ½ cup
- Baking powder – 1 tablespoon
- Salt, a pinch

Wet:
- Coconut milk – 1 can-14 ounces
- Agave nectar – 3 tablespoons
- Ground flaxseeds – 1 tablespoon mixed with warm water 2 tablespoons
- Lemon extract – 1 teaspoon
- Vanilla extract – ½ teaspoon
- Lemon zest – 1 teaspoons

Method
Grease your 3-4 quart slow cooker.

In a large bowl, mix flour, shredded coconut, coconut milk, nectar, salt, lemon extract, vanilla extract and flaxseeds. Combine well.

Pour the mixture in a cooker. Then sprinkle lemon zest evenly on the top. Stir the batter a little with a fork. Cook on high for 1-1 2/ hours until the pancake center is set.

Pumpkin coffee cake oatmeal

A simple breakfast dish that brings in a flavorful twist to the regular oatmeal. Healthy and tasty, the recipe will be loved by all critics.

Serves: 2 to 3

Ingredients
- Steel cut oats – ½ cup
- Unsweetened almond milk – 2 cups
- Vanilla extract – ½ tsp
- Pumpkin, chopped – ½ cup
- Cinnamon powder – ½ tsp

For topping
- Sweetener of your choice or brown sugar – 3 tbsp
- Cinnamon powder – ½ tsp
- Walnuts or pecans, chopped – 3 tbsp

Method
Mix all the ingredients and cook in a slow cooker for 7 to 9 hours on low. (Best left overnight). Stir and add the coffee cake topping. Serve warm or cooled.

Pear rose cardamom cake oatmeal

A soothing and yummy breakfast oatmeal that makes you forget everything else and simply enjoy. The ultimate comfort food for the soul that will make your day.

Serves: 2 to 3

Ingredients
- Steel cut oats – ½ cup
- Unsweetened coconut milk – 2 cups
- Pear, chopped -1
- Vanilla extract – ½ tsp
- Rosewater – ½ tsp
- Almond extract – ¼ tsp
- Cardamom powder – ¼ tsp
- Cinnamon powder – ¼ tsp
- Sweetener of your choice

Method
Mix all the ingredients, except the sweetener, and cook in a slow cooker for 7 to 9 hours on low (best left overnight to cook). Stir in the sweetener and serve warm or cooled.

Maple pear walnut cake oatmeal

The perfect oatmeal that will kick start your day with a bang. Packed with energy and great taste, this breakfast is bound to receive high acclaims from one and all.

Serves: 2 to 3

Ingredients
- Steel cut oats – ½ cup
- Unsweetened coconut milk – 2 cups
- Vanilla extract – ½ teaspoon
- Maple extract – ½ teaspoon
- Pear, chopped - 1
- Sweetener of your choice
- Walnuts, chopped – ¼ cup (for topping)
- Grated nutmeg – a pinch (for topping)

Method
Mix all the ingredients except sweetener and toppings and cook in a slow cooker for 7 to 9 hours on low. (Best left overnight). Stir and mix in the sweetener and add the toppings as desired. Serve warm or cooled.

Autumn fruity butter

How about having your crispy bread in the morning with a spiced combo of pumpkin, apple and pear? Yes, it's a fall butter recipe!

Makes: 6-8 cups

Ingredients
- Pears – 6 large, peeled, cored and chopped
- Apple – 4 large, peeled, cored and chopped
- Fresh pumpkin – 2 cups, cubed
- Juice from 2 lemons
- Agave nectar – ½ cup
- Cinnamon – 1 teaspoon
- Allspices, cardamom, ground ginger – ½ teaspoon each
- Ground cloves – ¼ teaspoon

Method:
Grease your 1-1 ½ quarts slow cooker. Place all the ingredients in it and leave its lid slightly opened with a ladle in the cooker. Cook on low for 8-10 hours to let all the liquid evaporate.

Let the mixture cool a bit and puree it in a blender in batches. Store in jars or freeze in plastic bags.

Orange-carrot cake with "Greek Yogurt" icing

This cake is a perfect oatmeal breakfast with a tanginess of orange and yogurt.

Serves: 2-3

Ingredients:
- Steel-cut oats – 1 /2 cup
- Orange juice – 1 cup
- Water – 1 cup
- Carrots – 2, chopped
- Cinnamon – ½ teaspoon
- Sweetener of your choice – as per taste

For icing:
- Greek yogurt – 1 container
- Walnuts – ¼ cup, chopped

Method

At night: grease your 1-1 ½ quarts slow cooker and place all the ingredients except icing and sweetener in it. Let them cook on low overnight.

In the morning: stir the contents well to adjust the consistency. Add the sweetener and mix well. Serve with a topping of a large scoop of yogurt chopped walnuts.

Apple oatmeal with white chocolate peanut butter

This is really a wonderful breakfast dish with sweet peanut butter coated apples and healthy oatmeal.

Serves: 2-3

Ingredients:
- Steel-cut oats – ½ cup
- Unsweetened milk – 2 cups
- Apple – 1, chopped
- White chocolate peanut butter – 2 tablespoons (look for only vegan peanut butter)
- Vanilla – ½ teaspoon

Method
At night: Grease your 1-1 ½ quarts slow cooker and add everything to it. Cook for 7-9 hours or whole night on low.

In the morning: Stir the oatmeal well to mix the water on top. Top it up with crushed peanuts and extra cut apples, if desired.

Pumpkin spice coconut sugar cashew creamer

It's a non-dairy creamer with a perfect consistency to make your latte wonderful, but no pumpkin at all!

Makes: 2 cups

Ingredients:
- Raw cashews – 1 cup
- Water – 1 ½ cups, for cooking
- Water – 2 cups, for blending
- Coconut sugar or any sweetener – ¼ cup+2 tablespoons
- Cinnamon – 1-2 tablespoons
- Allspice – 2 teaspoons
- Nutmeg and cloves – ¼ teaspoon each
- Salt, a pinch

Method

Take a 1-1 ½ quarts cooker. Put cashews and cooking water in it and cook on high for 3-4 hours. Then remove the cashews from the cooker and drain the water. Again, take water for blending, add cashews, spices and sweetener. Blend the mixture until smooth and creamy. Use the paste as creamer or add more water, if you like runny creamer.

Spiced creamer with date and apple

Another vegan, non-dairy creamer with cinnamon flavor, marvelously swathed up in coconut milk.

Makes: 1 pint

Ingredients:
- Coconut milk – 1 can
- Apple – 1 large, peeled and diced
- Dates – 8 small
- Cinnamon sticks – 4 whole
- Allspice – 1/8 teaspoon

Method:
Put everything in 1-1/2 quarts cooker and cook on low for 8 hours and on low for 4 hours. Before blending, remove the cinnamon sticks and make a smooth paste. Store in a container in the fridge. Use as and when required.

Crock pot molasses gingerbread latte

A dash of molasses and spicy flavor of molasses will give you a nicely brewed coffee in a chilly morning.

Serves: 2

Ingredients:
- Regular brewed coffee – 1 cup
- Unsweetened coconut milk – 2 cups
- Ground ginger – ½ teaspoon
- Cinnamon – ¼ teaspoon
- Ground allspice – 1/8 teaspoon
- Ground cloves, ground nutmeg – a pinch of each
- Molasses – 1 teaspoon
- Sweetener of your choice, to taste

Method
In a 3 quarts slow cooker, put all the ingredients and cook on high for 1 ½ hours or for 3 hours on low. Enjoy it piping hot.

Vanilla fig oatmeal with baklava topping

A delicious breakfast dish that infuses different flavors of the world in one bowl. It makes you enjoy oatmeal like never before.

Serves: 2 to 3

Ingredients:
- Steel cut oats – ½ cup
- Unsweetened non-dairy milk- 2 cups
- Dried figs, chopped - 2 cups
- Ground cardamom – ¼ teaspoon
- Orange flower water – ¼ teaspoon
- Vanilla extract – 1 teaspoon

For topping
- Chopped walnuts, pistachio & almonds – 1 tablespoon each
- Pinch of cardamom powder
- Sweetener of your choice

Method
Mix all the ingredients and cook in a slow cooker for 7 to 9 hours on low. Stir and add the toppings. Serve warm or cooled.

Morning caramel mocha with a dash of salt

With fat-free caramel and sugar-free chocolate syrup, this mocha is definitely a guilt-free delight!

Serves: 3-4

Ingredients:
For caramel:
- Pitted dates – 15, chopped
- Unsweetened non-dairy milk – 1 cup
- Vanilla – 1 teaspoons
- Salt, a pinch (optional)

Method:
Blend everything to make a smooth paste. If your blender is not powerful enough, cook everything for just 15 minutes to soften the dates. Cool and then blend.

For Chocolate syrup:
- Cocoa – ½ cup
- Water – ½ cup
- Sweetener – ½- 1 teaspoon
- Vanilla extract – ½ teaspoon

Method
In 1-1 ½ quarts slow cooker, add everything and cook on high for 1 hour, stirring in between. Check the consistency. It should be like a thick syrup. Remove from the cooker.

Store in the fridge for some time. Add 1 tablespoon of each, caramel and syrup in your cup of hot coconut milk to have a vegan mocha!

Oatmeal with sweetened date caramel topping

Complete nutrition in breakfast with hearty oatmeal having a gooey date topping!

Serves: 2-3

Ingredients:
For oatmeal
- Steel-cut oats – ½ cup
- Unsweetened coconut milk – 2 cups
- Shredded coconut – ¼ cup
- Vanilla extract – 1 teaspoon
- Sweetener of your choice, to taste

For topping:
- Shredded coconut – 2 tablespoons
- Date caramel – as in Recipe 9 above

Method
At night: Grease your 1-1 ½ quarts slow cooker. Add everything except sweetener and cook for the whole night on low.

In the morning: Stir in sweetener and adjust the consistency of oatmeal. Serve hot with a topping of date caramel and shredded coconut.

Coconut banana pecan coffee cake oatmeal

A tasty breakfast dish that brings about a twist to your daily oatmeal.

Serves: 2 to 3

Ingredients
- Steel cut oats – ½ cup
- Unsweetened coconut milk – 2 cups
- Coconut, shredded – 1/3 cup
- Banana, mashed - 1
- Vanilla extract – ½ teaspoon
- Coconut extract (optional) – ½ teaspoon
- Pecans, chopped
- Sweetener of your choice

Method
Mix oats, coconut, milk and extracts and cook in a slow cooker for 7 to 9 hours on low. (Best left overnight). Stir and mix in banana, sweetener and top with pecans. Serve warm or cooled.

Crockpot steel cut oatmeal

This delicious and spicy breakfast dish is the perfect serving of wholesome goodness that gives you the necessary energy boost for the day ahead. Best enjoyed warm.

Ingredients
- Steel cut oats – 2/3 cup
- Water – 3 cups
- Salt – to taste
- All spice powder – ¼ teaspoon
- Cardamom powder – ¼ teaspoon
- Cinnamon stick - 1
- Brown sugar or sweetener of your choice – 2 tablespoon
- Earth balance – 2 tablespoon
- Pinch of crushed pepper (optional)

Method
Add all the ingredients in the crockpot, stir and cook for 7-9 hours on low. (Best left overnight to cook). Remove cinnamon and serve. Best served with some fresh berries.

Soup Recipes

Healthy, soul-soothing and filling soup recipes I have picked for you in this section. You can serve these soups with a hearty salad or a delectable sandwich or a simple garlic bread will do. Having a soup ready in a slow cooker with aromatic ingredients is really comforting when you reach home after an appointment at the hospital or after a long walk in a cool breeze. Moreover, you can prepare soup in bulk and freeze it too!

Get-well-soon vegan slow cooker Chickpea soup

You'll love this soup, especially when you feel slightly under the weather. It's a game changer soup that will definitely soothe your coughing throat. Sip it hot and you'll probably like to have more next day. So, fill your crockpot with extra ingredients to make soup in bulk.

Here Kamut grain is used that usually takes more time to cook, but slow cooker is perfect for it. Also the yeast used here is highly nutritional to enhance health in soup with B vitamins, but use it as per availability at home.

Serves: 6

Ingredients:
- Chickpeas – 1 can (15.5 ounce)
- Celery – 1 cup chopped
- Turnip – 1 cup chopped
- Carrot – 1 cup chopped
- Kamut – ½ cup
- Garlic – 5-6 cloves, minced
- Water – 6 cups
- Vegetable bouillon – 2 cubes or 2 tablespoons
- Bay leaves – 2
- Dried thyme – 1 teaspoon
- Fresh rosemary – 1 sprig (2")

- Nutritional yeast (optional) – 2 tablespoons
- Salt and pepper – to taste

Method

Note: Use a 4-quart slow cooker

In a slow cooker, put all the ingredients except salt and pepper, nutritional yeast. Let the ingredients cook on high for 4-5 hours or 8-10 hours on low. Remove rosemary stem and bay leaves before serving. Season with salt and pepper and serve hot!

Crockpot vegan artichoke soup with soy 'sausages'

If you do not want your meal to be a knock-off for vegans, you must include this stuffed artichoke soup that is a comforting start before digging into a hearty vegan meal. A dash of vegan cheese adds flavor and creaminess to the soup.
It's a slightly lengthy recipe with various steps so be careful to get it right!

Serves: 6

Ingredients
For soup
- Onion – 1 chopped
- Carrot- 1 medium, chopped
- Celery – 2 stalks
- Garlic – 4 cloves minced
- Fennel seeds – ½ teaspoon
- Dried oregano -1/2 teaspoon
- Dried thyme – ½ teaspoon
- Dried rosemary – ½ teaspoon
- Garlic powder – ½ teaspoon
- Salt and pepper – to taste
- A dash of rep chilli flakes
- Artichoke hearts – 4 cans 14 ounces each, drained and chopped roughly
- Vegetable broth (low sodium) – 5 cups, divided

To make sausages:
- Soy curls – ½ cup, soaked in water for 10 minutes
- Garlic – 1 clove, chopped
- Garlic powder – 1 teaspoon
- Rubbed sage – 1 teaspoon
- Sweet paprika – ½ teaspoon
- Dried oregano – ½ teaspoon
- Fennel seeds – ½ teaspoon
- Black pepper – ¼ teaspoon
- Salt – a pinch

- Dry red wine – 1-2 tablespoons

For vegan cheese
- Raw cashews - ½ cup soaked in vegetable broth (low sodium) ½ cup
- Garlic powder – ½ teaspoon
- Nutritional yeast – ½ tablespoon
- Lemon juice from ½ lemon

Method
To prepare soup, take a 4 quart slow cooker and add all soup ingredients in it. Turn cooker on low and let the soup simmer for around 8 hours. Once it is made, let it cool at room temperature before blending it. Either use a stick blender in the cooker itself or divide the soup and churn it in blender. Do not make a smooth paste, but leave some artichoke chunks in it.

Now make sausages by draining soy curls and put them all in food processor's bowl. Add all spices and give 5-6 pulse to crush the curls. Heat a pan, drizzle some oil or vegetable broth, if you want a no-oil version. Put the sausage mixture into the pan and sauté until fragrant and begin to brown. Once the sausages are cooked, remove the pan from stove and deglaze using red wine. Keep aside the sausages to add into the soup while serving.

Prepare cheese by blending cashews with broth to make a fine, pourable paste. Add lemon juice, garlic powder and nutritional yeast to flavor the cheese. Blend again at high speed. Add little water or broth if you need to adjust the consistency of cheese.
While serving, reheat the soup, divide equally in 4-6 bowls, add sausages to each bowl and drizzle cheese over the top. Slurrp it and enjoy!

Quick and simple thick tomato soup

This one is for a lazy weekend evening when you are not in a mood to cook something lavish. The thickness of this soup will make you drool! But it's vegan so I carefully chose the ingredients to add creaminess to this filling soup. We have used cashews and oats to make it thick and extra delicious.

No doubt that it looks like regular condensed soups, but free from artificial preservatives and corn flour. So, give yourself a healthy and easy treat!

Serves: 6

Ingredients:
- Tomatoes - 1 can of 28 ounce, crush the canned tomatoes or you can use tomato purée
- Whole tomatoes – 1 can of 28 ounce, peeled
- Water - 3 cups
- Cashew pieces – ½ cup
- Oats (Scottish or steel-cut or rolled) – 3 tablespoons
- Vegetarian bouillon cubes – 1-2
- Dried basil – 1 tablespoon
- Garlic – 4 cloves
- Agave nectar (optional) – 1-2 tablespoon
- Salt and pepper to taste

Method

Use a 4 quart slow cooker. Add everything except salt and pepper, agave nectar to the cooker. Put cooker on low and cook for 8-10 hours. Let the soup cool before blending.

Divide it in 2 batches and blend soup until smooth. Season with salt and pepper as per your taste and add agave nectar, if using. Reheat soup, if desired and enjoy it!

Oil-free slow cooker vegan white bean soup

This is a really 'veganized' soup having the sweetness of agave nectar, instead of honey, and you can leave it in a slow cooker to have when you reach home after a long day. How about having a delicious, crunchy oat bread with soup to make a complete meal?

Servings: 6

Ingredients:
- Dry cannellini or great northern beans – 1 ½ cups
- Water with 2 vegetarian bouillon cubes or vegetable broth – 8 cups
- Carrots – 3 medium, diced
- Sweet potato – 1 cup, diced
- Diced tomatoes – 1 -14.5 oz.
- Bay leaves – 2
- Basil – 1 teaspoon
- Marjoram – 1 teaspoon
- Fresh rosemary – 2 sprigs or you can use dried rosemary – ½ teaspoon
- Pepper and salt to taste
- Agave nectar – 1-2 teaspoon

Method:
In a 4-5 quart crockpot, put all the ingredients except pepper and salt, agave nectar. Turn on the slow cooker at low and let the ingredients cook for 7-9 hours. When done, add agave nectar and seasonings. Serve it hot with bread of your choice.

Delicious vegan split pea and farro soup

If you want to have a steaming bowl of healthy vegan soup with garlicky, cheezy croutons on the top, then follow this recipe and you are all set.

Serves: 6-8

Ingredients:
- Plain farro – 1 ½ cups
- Vegetable bouillon cubes – 2
- Split peas – 1 cup
- Water – 8 cups
- Bay leaves – 3
- Potato or turnip – 2 cups, chopped
- Smoked paprika – 2 teaspoon
- Turmeric – 1 teaspoon
- Dried oregano or any herb of your choice – ½ teaspoon
- Pepper and salt to taste
- Bread pieces – for croutons
- Olive oil – to drizzle
- Garlic powder – 1 teaspoon

Method
If you are out of the house for around 8-9 hours, then cook it on low in a slow cooker, but if you want to have the soup as supper and do not have enough time then cook on high for 3-4 hours. Use a 4 quart cooker and add everything except pepper and salt.

Let the soup cook. To make croutons, cut bread pieces into 2" pieces. Drizzle some olive oil on an oven-proof plate and spread bread pieces over it. Sprinkle garlic powder and let cook for 7 minutes at 350 degrees.

While serving, reheat the soup as per your choice and serve with croutons.

Corn cabbage vegan slow cooker soup

This soup is a complete mind changer for picky eaters. Even those who have an intense disliking for cabbage will love it. This recipe is surely a keeper!

This recipe requires little preparation a night before.

Serves: 4

Ingredients:
- Onion – ½ small, minced
- Garlic – 2 cloves, minced
- Ginger – 2-3 teaspoons, minced
- Mushrooms – 1 ½ cups, minced
- Cabbage – 4 cups, chopped
- Corn kernels – 2 cups (frozen or fresh)
- Olive oil (optional, you can use water to sauté) – 1 tablespoon
- Water – 4 cups
- Salt – a pinch
- Vegan bouillon – 2 teaspoons
- Sesame oil – 1 teaspoon
- Sriracha sauce – ½-1 teaspoon
- Light soy sauce – 1 teaspoon

Method
Prepare mushroom mixture a night before to save time. Drizzle a pan with oil or water, as desired. Sauté onion few minutes until translucent, then add minced garlic to the pan and saute for one more minute. Now put mushrooms in pan and sprinkle salt over it. Let the mushroom release its water and cook thoroughly. Remove this mixture from pan and store in a container. Mix cut cabbage and corns in it and keep in the fridge for the whole night.

In the morning, turn on slow cooker and put all the soup ingredients, mushroom-cabbage mixture except sriracha sauce and soy sauce in it. Cook on low temperature for 8-9 hours. Your delicious soup will be ready after a long simmer. Enjoy it with a dash of soy sauce, sriracha sauce and seasoning, if liked.

Feel good Okra-corn soup

With this soup, you won't feel sick and your energy will boost up. Having okra and corn, this amazing dish will make a hearty dinner with a piece of garlic dinner and some healthy salad. If you are really tired and dozed up, then you can skip onion from the recipe so that you don't have to stand in front of stove to sauté it. You can simply throw all the ingredients in a crockpot and rest. Your soup will be ready within 8-9 hours in a slow cooker.

Serves: 6

Ingredients:
- Onion – ½ medium, minced
- Green pepper – ½ medium, minced
- Garlic – 3 cloves, minced
- Olive oil (optional) – 2 tablespoons
- Vegetable broth – 3 cups or you can use 2 vegan bouillon cubes dissolved in water
- Frozen okra (sliced) – 1 x 16 oz bag
- Frozen corn kernels - 2 cups (11 oz)
- Plain or fire roasted crushed tomatoes – 1 can (28 oz)
- Smoked paprika – ½ teaspoon
- Oregano, thyme and marjoram – 1 teaspoon each
- Cayenne pepper (grounded) – ¼-1/2 teaspoon
- Pepper and salt to taste

Method
If you are adding onion, then you need to sauté them first in a pan with a little olive oil or water, as liked. Let onion become translucent. Now turn on your slow cooker on low temperature and put all the ingredients except salt and pepper in it. Let everything cook for 8-9 hours or you can turn your cooker at high for 4-5 hours, if you need the soup early. Season your soup with salt and pepper and sip it!

Vegan fall season lentil soup

The colorful lentils used in this soup give a delighting effect to your mood and this soup is a perfect accompaniment for a light meal of sumptuous salad and whole wheat bread. Moreover, it is gluten-free, so enjoy it wholeheartedly.

Serves: 4

Ingredients:
- Olive oil -1 tablespoon
- Onion – ½ small, chopped
- Garlic – 2 cloves, minced
- Lentils – 1 cup
- Water – 5 cups
- Potato – 2 cups, chopped
- Carrot – 1, chopped
- Celery – 1 stalk, minced
- Bouillon – 1 tablespoon
- Fresh rosemary – 1 sprig or you can use 1/4 teaspoon grounded
- Fresh thyme – 1 sprig or 1 teaspoon dried
- Plain salt or smoked salt and pepper to taste

Method
Prepare onion mixture by sautéing onion and garlic lightly in olive oil a night before.

Store this mixture in refrigerator overnight with other cut veggies. In the morning, put all veggies and onion mixture in a slow cooker. Turn cooker on low temperature and leave it for 8-9 hours. Take pleasure in the soup with seasonings on the top.

Thick and hearty split pea soup

It's a delightful soup when you are running low on your monthly budget and don't have much in your pantry. With less costly ingredients, you can dish up this hearty soup to fill your appetite!

Serves: 2-3

Ingredients:
- Water – 3 cups
- Bouillon cube – 1
- Dry split peas – 1 cup
- Potato – 1 cup, diced
- Bay leaves – 2
- Turmeric – 1 teaspoon
- Thyme – 1 teaspoon
- Grounded rosemary – ¼ teaspoon or regular rosemary – ½ teaspoon
- Pepper and salt to taste

Method
Use a 1 ½- 2 quarts slow cooker. Turn it on low temperature and add all the ingredients into the cooker except pepper and salt. Let the ingredients cook for 7-10 hours. Adjust seasoning before serving. You can have it with toasted bread dunked in it.

For storing the leftover, you may add little water to the soup as it may get thicker once stored in the refrigerator.

Veggie soup with toasted pecans

This is a year round favorite soup that lets you have the goodness of veggies with the flavors of aromatic herbs and the tanginess of cider vinegar. Serve it with toasted pecans on top to make the dish more sumptuous.

Serves: 2

Ingredients:
- Water – 2 cups
- Winter squash – 1 ½ cups, diced
- Brussels sprouts – 1 cup, shredded
- Carrots – ½ cup diced
- Bell pepper – ¼ cup, diced
- Onion – 2 tablespoons, sautéed in a little oil
- Garlic – 1 clove, minced
- Vegan Bouillon cube – 1
- Dried sage – 1 teaspoon
- Dried thyme – 2 teaspoons
- Apple cider vinegar – 1 teaspoon
- Salt and pepper to taste

For garnishing, you may need toasted pecans, lightly minced (optional).

Method
For this recipe, you need a 1 ½- 2 quarts slow cooker.

Add everything in the cooker except salt, pepper and vinegar. Cook on low temperature for about 7-9 hours.

While serving, add a dash of cider vinegar to each soup bowl and sprinkle salt and pepper to taste.

Top it with toasted pecans and relish your veggie soup!

Veggies and Cranberry beans soup

With an Italian flavor, this soup will surely tickle your taste buds. Throw in veggies, beans herbs and vinegar to make a filling soup.

Serves: 6

Ingredients:
- Dried Cranberry beans – 1 ½ cups or you can use white navy beans or any other dried beans except kidney beans
- Water – 6 cups
- Vegan bouillon cube – 1
- Celery – 1 cup, diced
- Carrot – 1 cup, diced or shredded
- Sweet potato – 1 cup, diced
- Onion – ½ cup, minced
- Garlic – 3 cloves, minced
- Balsamic vinegar – 1 tablespoon
- Thyme – 1 teaspoon
- Basil, marjoram -1 teaspoon each
- Rosemary, oregano – ½ teaspoon each
- Tomatoes – 1 can (15.5 oz), diced
- Nutritional yeast – ¼ cup
- Salt and pepper to taste
- Greens (optional) – 1-2 handfuls, chopped)

Method
In a bowl, soak dry beans in enough water and keep overnight. In the morning, take a 4 quart slow cooker and fill it with all the ingredients except tomatoes, yeast, salt, pepper and greens.

Cook on low temperature for 8-9 hours.

Nutritional yeast and tomatoes you can add just half an hour before serving. When you add the tomatoes and yeast almost after 8 hours, turn the cooker on high and cook for 20-30 minutes.

Add greens either in the cooker or individually in each bowl. The greens would not take time to cook as it will soften with warmth of soup.

Adjust seasoning and serve.

Note: You may add more herbs before serving to adjust the flavor.

Hot and sour Chinese vegan soup

You might be having a hard time finding a vegan version of hot and sour soup in Chinese restaurants. So, why not cook your own? Tofu here will make you go crazy for this soup.

Serves: 3-4

Ingredients:
- Silken or regular tofu – 1 packet, cubed
- Vegetarian broth with 1 teaspoon nutritional yeast – 2 cups
- Water – 2 cups
- Vegan bouillon – 1 tablespoon
- Button mushrooms – ½ packet, sliced
- Dried shitakes – 8
- Bamboo shoots – 1 can, thinly striped
- Garlic – 3 cloves, crushed or minced
- Fresh ginger – 2 tablespoons, grated (no ginger powder at all!)
- Soy sauce – 1 tablespoon
- Sesame oil – 1 teaspoon
- Chili paste – 1 teaspoon
- Rice wine vinegar – 2 tablespoons
- Fresh or frozen peas – 1 ½ cups

Method
You can chop, mince or cube veggies and other stuff at night to cut your preparation time in the morning.

In the morning, fill your 4 quart slow cooker with all the ingredients except peas. Let the cooker be on low temperature and leave it for 8 hours.

Before serving, stir in peas. Adjust the taste by adding little more chili paste and vinegar.

You can also serve chili sauce to allow your guests to add to the hot soup!

Sweet potato curried lentil slow cooker soup

It's a flavorful, rich soup that will fill your home with awesome fragrance of curried lentils simmering in a slow cooker. It will fill your appetite too!

Serves: 4-6

Ingredients:
- Onion - 1 medium, diced
- Garlic – 3 cloves, minced
- Sweet potato – 1 large, diced into ½" cubes
- Dried brown lentils – 1 ½ cups
- Tomatoes - 1-14 oz. can diced
- Vegetable broth - 6 cups
- Coconut milk - 1 cup
- Fresh ginger - ½ tablespoon, grated
- Asian chili paste - ½ tablespoon (or to taste)
- Ground cumin – 2 tablespoons
- Salt – 1 teaspoon
- Pepper – ½ teaspoon
- Lime juice – 2 tablespoons (about 1 lime)
- Fresh cilantro - ¼ cup, chopped

Method
In a 4 quart slow cooker, add everything except cilantro and lime juice. Using a ladle, mix all the ingredients well. Turn on cooker at low temperature and cook for 5-6 hours. Your lentils and sweet potato will soften and curried thoroughly in these long hours. Serve it hot with a dash of lime juice and cilantro on top.

Stuffed pepper slow cooker soup

Looking for a yummy dinner option but do not want to spend all day in the kitchen? Try this simple slow cooker vegan recipe with a few minutes of preparation and all you will be set!

Serves: 8

Ingredients:
- Olive oil – 1 teaspoon
- Onion – 1 diced
- Celery – 2 ribs, diced
- Carrot – 2 small, diced
- Garlic – 3-5 cloves, minced
- Tempeh – 1 pound, grated
- Green bell pepper – 1 large of 2 small, diced
- Red bell pepper - 1 large of 2 small, diced
- Fire-roasted tomatoes – 2-15 ounce cans, diced
- Vegetable broth – 32 ounces
- Uncooked brown rice – 1 cup
- Water – 2 ½ cups
- Salt – 1 ½ teaspoon
- Pepper – 1 teaspoon

Method
You can do all the preparations for the soup at night to save some time the next day. In a pan, add olive oil and sauté onion, carrot and celery until everything becomes soft. Add tempeh and garlic and cook until the tempeh turns brown.

In a 4-5 quarts slow cooker, put vegetable and tempeh mixture along with other ingredients and cook on high temperature for 4-5 hours and 8-9 hours on low temperature. Bon appetite!

Kale and sweet potato slow cooker soup

It can be called a super-nutritious dish with healthy food like kale and sweet potato.a Packed with essential vitamins and other nutrients, this soup is a wonder item in your meal, especially for women health.

Serves: 6

Ingredients:
- Extra virgin olive oil – 1 tablespoon
- Red onion – ½ small, diced
- Garlic – 2 cloves, minced
- Red bell pepper – ½ cup, diced
- Sweet potatoes – 2, peeled and cubed
- Red pepper flakes – ¼ teaspoon
- Paprika – 1 teaspoon
- Sea salt to taste
- Bay leaf – 1
- Low sodium, fat-free vegetable stock – 2 ½ cups
- Kale – 1 cup, rinsed

Method
In a pan, drizzle olive oil and stir-fry onion and garlic until soften. Take a 4 quart slow cooker. Keep aside kale and put all other ingredients along with onion-garlic in it. Cook on low temperature for 6-8 hours. Just 10 minutes before serving, add kale to cooker and let it wilt. Serve while removing bay leaves.

Appetizers and side dishes to complement your meal!

If you want to enjoy chip'n dip while watching a movie or having a casual get-together with your vegan friends, then this section is for you. It also contains side dishes to spruce up your dining table. Whether its rice or veggies stir-fried, a side dish always supplements your lavish main dishes.

Nutmeg spiced vegan ricotta and spinach dip

If you want to adorn your dish with 'fake cheese', then vegan ricotta is the best. This dip is lighter than the original cheezy one and has immense nutrition.

Serves: 2

Ingredients:
- Spinach – 1 ¼ cup
- Canned butter beans – 6 cups, drained
- Tofu – ½ cup, drained
- Soy cream – 3 tablespoons
- Almond milk – 3 tablespoons
- Ground nutmeg – 1 teaspoon
- Nutritional yeast – 1 tablespoon
- Dijon mustard – ½ teaspoon
- Garlic – 1 clove, grated
- Salt and pepper, as per taste

Method
In a 4 quart slow cooker, add everything except spinach. Cook on low for 6-8 hours. Add spinach when 30 minutes left for the end of cooking time. Let the spinach wilt and mix well. Adjust seasoning before serving with your choice of chips.

Vegan 'Velveeta' cheese dip

Similar to original velveeta dip, this 'Veganeeta' can be combined well with salsa to add spice to your meal.

Serves: 3-4

Ingredients:
- Raw cashews – ½ cup
- Tahini – 1 tablespoon
- Lemon juice – ½ tablespoon
- Apple cider vinegar – 2 teaspoons
- Unsweetened coconut milk – 1 cup + 1-3 tablespoons
- Water – ¼ cup
- Sea salt – ½ teaspoon
- Prepared yellow mustard – ¼ teaspoon
- Arrowroot powder – 1 tablespoon
- Paprika – ½ teaspoon
- Turmeric – 1/8 teaspoon
- Nutritional yeast – 1- 1 ½ teaspoon (optional)

Method
Combine all the ingredients in a 1-1 ½ quarts slow cooker and cook for either 1 hour on high or 2 hours on low. Stir the sauce well and adjust seasonings. Dip tortilla chips and enjoy!

Vegan salsa Verde

Now your nacho bar will be 'all vegan' with his Salsa Verde that turn out smooth and perfect in a slow cooker!

Makes: 2 cups

Ingredients:
- Tomatillos – 15 whole, peeled
- Sweet onion – ½ medium, chopped
- Garlic – 1-2 cloves, chopped
- Jalapeno – 1, seeded and cup
- Lime – 1, juiced
- Fresh cilantro – 1 cup
- Salt, to taste

Method
Combine everything in a 1-1 ½ quarts slow cooker and cook for 1 hour on high or 2 hours on low. Let it cool and then blend until smooth. Adjust seasoning and chill in the fridge before serving.

Thai salad with tofu in pineapple & barbeque sauce

A delicious salad that is high in taste and flavor and very low in salt and sugar. Best served with fresh salad greens.

Serves: 6

Ingredients
- Tofu, defrosted – 2 packets
- Onion, chopped – 1 large
- Garlic, minced – 8 cloves
- Chile peppers, crushed - 2
- Ginger root, peeled and minced – 2 inch piece
- Dates, deseeded – ½ cup
- Pineapple, crushed – 1 ½ cup
- Water – 1/3 cup
- Tomato paste – 5 tablespoon
- Light soy sauce – 2 tablespoon
- Lemon juice – 2 tablespoon
- Cider vinegar – 1 tablespoon
- Pepper to taste
- Salt to taste (optional)

Method
Freeze tofu a day before cooking, defrost, squeeze out the water and cut into cubes. Saute onion and garlic in oil. Cool and blend with all other ingredients except tofu. Pour sauce over tofu in the slow cooker and cook for 8 hours on low. Serve with salad greens.

Summer pasta sauce with fresh basil

A perfect choice to beat the heat, this flavorful sauce that can bring about a yummy twist in your regular pasta. The sauce can be stored in the freezer.

Ingredients
- Olive oil – 1 tablespoon
- Medium sized onion, minced – 1/2
- Bell pepper, minced – ½ cup
- Eggplants, diced – 2 cups
- Italian tomatoes, chopped – 3 cups
- Diced tomatoes – 2 cans
- Dried oregano – 1 teaspoon
- Fresh basil, chopped- ¼ cup
- Salt to taste
- Pepper to taste

Method
Saute the onion and bell peppers in heated oil and take out in a bowl. Add the eggplant and diced tomatoes to the bowl, cover and leave overnight.

Cook all the ingredients along with the overnight mixture in the slow cooker for 4 hours at high. Season with salt and pepper and mix in the fresh basil.. Can be served chunky or pureed. Pour over pasta and serve.

Vegan hot and cheezy corn dip

This sauce is a great addition to your appetizer repertoire, which you can spread on tortillas, nachos or simply toss with your pasta.

Serves: 3-4

Ingredients:
- Sweet corns – 2 cans, well drained
- Jalapenos – 1-2 small, cut
- Vegan mozzarella cheese – 2 cups, shredded
- Nutritional yeast – 3-4 cups, grounded
- Vegan mayonnaise – 1 cup
- Salt and pepper, to taste

Method
Add everything except mayo and salt and pepper to 1-1 ½ quarts slow cooker. Cook on low for 1 hour. Remove sauce from cooker and add mayonnaise, adjust seasoning and serve.

Caramelized leeks with pureed lentils

It's a healthy dip with the goodness of leeks and lentils that you can enjoy with pita chips.

Serves: 3-4

Ingredients:
- Brown lentils – 1 cup, soaked in water for 2 hours
- Leeks – ¼ cup (both green and white parts)
- Lemon zest – 1 tablespoon
- Olive oil – 2 tablespoon
- Garlic powder – ½ teaspoon
- Sea salt – ¼ teaspoon

Pita chips – 2 ounces

Method

At night: In a 4 quart slow cooker, add the lentils and ½ teaspoon salt. Cook on low overnight.

In the morning: In a pan, sauté leeks with 1 tablespoon olive oil and a pinch of salt. Let them caramelize in the pan. Remove cooked lentils from the cooker, let them cool, then puree in a blender until smooth.

In a bowl, mix olive oil, garlic powder, lemon zest and sea salt. While serving the dip, arrange leeks over it and pour flavored oil. Enjoy with pita chips!

Crock pot caramelized carrots

Wonderfully glazed carrots look yummy. It makes a great appetizer to boost your appetite!

Serves: 4

Ingredients:
- Baby carrots – 6-8, peeled
- Orange marmalade – 6 tablespoons
- Water – 1 tablespoon
- Olive oil – 3 tablespoons
- Salt and pepper, as per taste

Method
Combine everything in a 1-1 ½ quarts slow cooker and cook on low for 7-9 hours. Serve warm with little parsley sprinkle on top.

Flavored courgette side dish

It's a great vegan side dish loaded with taste and health both. With a dash of dry oregano, it tastes yummy!

Serves: 4

Ingredients:
- Courgette – 7-8 pieces, cut into rounds
- Red pepper – 1, chopped
- Onion – 2, chopped
- Garlic – 2 cloves, chopped
- Plum tomatoes – 5, chopped
- Olive oil – 2 tablespoons
- Fresh basil – a handful, chopped
- Salt and pepper, to taste
- Dry oregano – ½ teaspoon

Method
In a 4 quart slow cooker, combine everything except basil and oregano. Cook for 2 hours on high temperature. Serve hot with basil and oregano sprinkled on top.

Slow cooker coconut rice in Thai-style

This rice dish has the subtle flavors that are prominent in Thai cuisine. Moreover, it can be eaten with stewed veggies or spicy chili.

Serves 4

Ingredients:
- Olive oil – 3 tablespoons
- Shallots – 3, thinly sliced
- Red chili – 1, seeded and minced
- Root ginger – 5 cm, minced
- Garlic – 1 clove, minced
- Thai Jasmine rice – 3 cups
- Lime zest – from 1 lime
- Ground nutmeg – a pinch
- Bay leaves – 2
- Coconut milk – 3 cups
- Water – 2 cups
- Salt and pepper to taste

For garnish
- Fresh coriander – 1 bunch, chopped
- Spring onion – 3 tablespoons, chopped

Method
In a pan, heat 2 tablespoons olive oil and stir-fry ginger, garlic and onion until tender.

Combine everything except the garnish ingredients in a 4 quart cooker. Cook on high for 2 hours. Stir after the first hour to let everything combine well. Serve with chopped coriander and spring onions on the top.

German-style vinegary potato salad

It's a great alteration of regular mayonnaise loaded potato salad. With a vinegary flavor and mustard dressing, this salad tastes best when served warm.

Serves 16

Ingredients:
- Cider vinegar – 1/3 cup
- Whole-grain mustard – 3 tablespoons
- All-purpose flour – 2 tablespoons
- Salt – ½ teaspoon
- Freshly ground pepper -1/2 teaspoon
- Potatoes – 3 pounds, cut lengthwise or cut in quarters, if big
- Celery – 2 cups, sliced
- Sweet onion – 1 medium, chopped
- Fresh dill – ¼ cups, chopped

Method

Prepare a dressing by mixing vinegar, mustard, flour, salt and pepper. Whisk well.

In a 5-6 quart slow cooker, combine potatoes, dressing, celery and onion. Cook for 5 hours on low until everything gets mixed well. Serve warm with a sprinkle of dill.

Crockpot Edamame munch

This slow cooker recipe allows Edamame to absorb all the flavors nicely to give you a kick start for a lavish meal!

Serves: 2-3

Ingredients:
- Crushed red chili flakes – ½ teaspoon
- Coarse salt – 1 teaspoon
- Sugar – ½ teaspoon
- Edamame beans with shells – 1 pound

Method

In a 4 quart slow cooker, combine beans, chili flakes, salt and sugar. Cook on low for 6-8 hours or until the beans are tender. Adjust seasoning before serving.

Lemony-gingery hot toddies

If you are under the weather, then have this hot toddy infused with ginger to get out of that chill.

Serves: 14

Ingredients:
- Water – 8 cups
- Fresh lemon juice – 2 cups
- Agave nectar – 2 cups
- Ginger – 5 tablespoons, finely chopped
- Fresh ginger – 3" inches piece cut into strips
- Iced tea – 1 ½ cup
- Lemon rind strips

Method
In a 4 ½ quart slow cooker, put the first 5 ingredients and cook for 4 hours on high. Discard ginger slices from the liquid.
Stir in iced tea and pour in mugs. Serve warm with lemon rind garnish.

Ginger-peach chunky sauce

Tangy, chunky sauce to be served as an accompaniment.

Makes: 4 ¼ cups

Ingredients:
- Onion - 2 cups, chopped
- Fresh or frozen peaches - 4 cups, peeled and sliced
- Golden raisins - 1 cup
- Firmly packed light brown sugar - 1 cup
- Crystallized ginger - 1/4 cup
- Mustard seeds - 1 teaspoon
- Ground ginger - 1/2 teaspoon
- Ground cinnamon - 1/4 teaspoon
- Ground cloves - 1/4 teaspoon
- All-purpose flour – 1.1 ounces (about 1/4 cup)
- Cider vinegar - 1/4 cup

Method
In a pan, stir-fry onion until tender.
In a 3 quart slow cooker, add everything except flour and vinegar.
In a bowl, mix vinegar and flour and add this mixture in the slow cooker. Cook for 5 hours on low heat.

Black-eyes peas with rice – Hoppin' John

Legend says this dish brings good luck on New Year, if eaten that day!

Serves: 6

Ingredients:
- Frozen black-eyed peas - 2 (16-ounce) packages
- Green onions - 1 1/4 cups, sliced, divided
- Hot water - 2 cups
- Red bell pepper - 3/4 cup, chopped
- Seeded jalapeño pepper - 2 tablespoons, minced
- Hot sauce - 2 teaspoons
- Salt - 1/4 teaspoon
- Freshly ground black pepper - 1/4 teaspoon
- Vegetable-flavored bouillon - 1 cube
- Diced tomatoes with pepper, celery, and onion - 1 (14.5-ounce) can, undrained
- Tomato paste - 1 tablespoon
- Uncooked converted rice - 2/3 cup

Method
In a 3 quarts slow cooker, add the first 9 ingredients with only ¾ green onions. Cook for 4 hours on high. After 3 hours, add rice, tomato paste and canned tomatoes. Stir well. Cook for 1 more hour until the water is absorbed. Stir rest of the onion and serve hot.

Lentil Quinoa Taco filling

A quick wrap that is healthy and tasty enough to satisfy even the most difficult health or food critic. Best enjoyed warm along with a cool drink.

Serves: 4

Ingredients
- Brown lentils – ¼ cup
- Quinoa – ¼ cup
- Water – 2 cups
- Garlic, minced – 2 cloves
- Chilli powder – ½ tsp
- Smoked paprika – ½ teaspoon
- Taco shells - 6
- Salt to taste
- Pepper to taste

Method
Add everything else in the slow cooker except salt, pepper and taco shells. Cook for 7 to 9 hours on low. Serve the filling in taco shells along with lettuce, tomato slices and any other topping of your choice.

Slow cooker Succotash

It's a true Mediterranean dish with olives, zucchini, beans and couscous. Interesting and healthy!

Serves: 8

Ingredients:
- Organic vegetable broth - 1 cup
- Zucchini - 1 cup, chopped
- Red bell pepper - 1 cup, chopped
- Pitted kalamata olives - 1/2 cup, halved
- Garlic - 2 cloves, minced
- Cannellini beans - 2 (15-ounce) cans, rinsed and drained
- Diced tomatoes - 1 (14.5-ounce) can, Undrained
- Fresh parsley - 1/4 cup, chopped
- Balsamic vinegar - 2 tablespoons
- Fresh lemon juice - 2 tablespoons
- Freshly ground black pepper - 1/4 teaspoon
- Couscous - 1 (10-ounce) package

Method
In a 3 quart slow cooker, combine the first 7 ingredients. Cook for 4 hours on low. Then stir in the remaining ingredients except couscous.

Prepare couscous according to the package instruction, but do not add fat and salt. Serve sucottash hot over couscous.

Fruity-lemonade tea

With fresh berries and lemonade, this drink will surely welcome your guests.

Serves: 12

Ingredients:
- Teas bags – 12
- Water – 8 cups
- Refrigerated natural lemonade – 5 cups
- Agave nectar – 1/3 cup
- Mixed berries – 1 (12 ounce) packet
- Lemons – 2, cut into 12 thin slices

Method
In a 3 quarts slow cooker, place tea bags without paper cover, water, and other ingredients except lemon slices. Strain lemonade and discard any solids. Pour over ice in each glass and serve with lemon wedges.

Orange lemon sipper

Sugary and spicy sipper to be served as a welcome drink.

Serves: 8

Ingredients:
- Apple juice – 6 cups
- Sugar – ¼ cup
- Cinnamon stick – 9 inches
- Cloves – 8 whole
- Anise seeds – ½ teaspoon
- Naval orange – 1 large, sliced
- Lemon – 1 medium, sliced

Method
In a 3 quart slow cooker, add everything except sliced lemon and orange. Cook for 2 hours on high. Then add lemon and orange slices. Cook for extra 30 minutes.

Strain the liquid and discard solids. Put again in the cooker on low to keep warm before serving.

Vegetable vegan cheese sauce

A yummy cheezy sauce that is bound to be loved by one and all. Tossed with pasta, this sauce makes the dish a perfect comfort food.

Serves: 3-4

Ingredients
- Cauliflower florets – 1 ½ cup
- Carrots, sliced – 1 cup
- Turnip, peeled and sliced – ½ cup
- Garlic, minced – 1 teaspoon
- Cashew – 1/3 cup
- Water – 2 ½ cups
- Unsweetened almond milk – 1 cup
- Nutritional yeast – ¼ cup
- Mustard powder – ¼ teaspoon
- Smoked paprika – ¼ teaspoon
- Salt to taste

Method
Cook the vegetables and cashew with water in a slow cooker for 7 to 9 hours on low to medium. Drain out and mix in the other ingredients. Blend until smooth consistency.

Best served with pasta, tossed along with sauted mushrooms or Mexican spices.

Crock pot pumpkin-cinnamon toddy

Sip it with your snacks and enjoy the hot sips!

Serves: 8

Ingredients:
- Water – 5 cups
- Pure maple syrup – ½ cup
- Canned pumpkin – 1/3 cup
- Cinnamon schnapps – ½ cup
- Ground cinnamon – to garnish

Method
Combine everything except ground cinnamon in a 3 ½ quarts slow cooker. Cook for 3-4 hours on low heat and 2 hours on high. Pour it in mugs and sprinkle ground cinnamon on each mug. Serve hot.

Crockpot tropical punch

Greet your guests with this tropical sipper. They will love your recipe!

Serves: 16

Ingredients:
- Orange-pineapple-banana juice – 5 cups
- Mango nectar – 2 cups
- Coconut water – 1 can-11 ounces
- Agave nectar – ¼ cup
- Lime peel – ½ teaspoon, shredded
- Allspice – 1 teaspoon
- Ginger ale – 2 bottles-12 ounces each
- Fresh or canned pineapple slices – 4 halves
- Lime juice – 2 tablespoons

Method
Combine the first 6 ingredients in a 3 ½ quart slow cooker. Cook on high for 2 hours or for 4 hours on low.

With a slotted spoon, remove allspice. Add pineapple, lime juice and ginger ale. Cook for another 15 minutes and serve warm.

Slow cooker rice with Cuban beans

It's an inexpensive dish with dried beans for a wholesome meal.

Serves: 10

Ingredients:
- Dried black beans – 1 pound
- Water – 2 cups
- Organic vegetable broth - 2 cups
- Onion – 2 cups, chopped
- Red bell pepper - 1 1/2 cups, chopped
- Green bell pepper - 1 cup, chopped
- Olive oil - 2 tablespoons
- Salt - 1 1/2 teaspoons
- Fennel seeds - 2 teaspoons, crushed
- Ground coriander - 2 teaspoons
- Ground cumin - 2 teaspoons
- Dried oregano - 2 teaspoons
- Diced tomatoes and green chiles - 2 (10-ounce) cans, drained
- Hot cooked rice - 5 cups
- Hot sauce (optional)

Method
Soak beans for at least 8 hours. In a 4 quart slow cooker, add everything except rice, and tomatoes. Cook for 5 hours on high. Serve on rice.

Vegan curried chickpeas with coconut milk

It's a great dish for your hearty meal that can be well eaten with a bowl of rice.

Serves: 3-4

Ingredients:
- Canola oil - 2 teaspoons
- Onion - 1 1/2 cups, chopped
- Garlic - 2 cloves, minced
- Chickpeas (garbanzo beans) - 2 (19-ounce) cans, rinsed and drained
- No-salt-added diced tomatoes - 2 (14.5-ounce) cans, undrained
- Light coconut milk - 1 (13.5-ounce) can
- Curry powder - 1 tablespoon
- Chopped pickled jalapeño pepper - 2 tablespoons
- Salt - 1 teaspoon
- Fresh cilantro - 1/2 cup, chopped
- Hot cooked basmati rice - 6 cups

Method
In a skillet, sauté onion and garlic in oil, until tender. Now in a 4 quart slow cooker, add everything except rice and cilantro. Cook for 6-8 hours on low. Top it up with cilantro and serve with rice.

Herbed rice with toasted nuts

This simple rice dish will spruce up your meal time.

Serves: 3-4

Ingredients:
- Vegan margarine - 3 tablespoons
- Uncooked converted long-grain rice - 1 3/4 cups
- Vegetable broth - 2 (14-ounce) cans
- Salt - 1/4 teaspoon
- Green onions – 6, chopped
- Dried basil - 1 teaspoon
- Pine nuts, toasted - 1/3 cup
- Garnish: fresh basil sprig

Method
In a skillet, stir- fry rice until brown and transfer to 4 quart slow cooker with other ingredients, except nuts and basil. Cook on high for 2 hours. Serve with fresh basil and pine nut topping.

Slow cooker glazed yams

An alternated version of Southern staple, this dish is an ideal accompaniment for your sumptuous main dishes.

Serves: 4-5

Ingredients:
- Vegan margarine - 1/4 cup
- Vanilla extract - 2 teaspoons
- Salt - 1/4 teaspoon
- Granulated sugar - 1 cup
- Firmly packed brown sugar - 1 cup
- Sweet potatoes - 4 pounds, peeled and cut into 1/2-inch-thick slices
- Cornstarch - 2 tablespoons

Method
Mix salt and vanilla with margarine. Combine both the sugars. In a 6 quart slow cooker, layer the potatoes. Pour the sugar and butter mixture on top and cook for 4 hours on low temperature. Using a slotted spoon, take out the potatoes on a serving plate, keeping the liquid inside the cooker.

Mix cornstarch in the cooker liquid. In a saucepan, heat a little water and add cornstarch mix. Boil for a minute and pour it over the potatoes. Serve warm.

Three pepper vegan bowl

Slightly sweet flavored relish that goes well with tacos!

Serves: 3-4

Ingredients:
- Yellow onion - 1 small, diced
- Distilled white vinegar - 1/2 cup
- Fresh lemon juice - 1/2 cup
- Sugar - 1/4 cup
- Kosher salt - 1 teaspoon
- Dried crushed red pepper - 1/4 teaspoon
- Yellow bell pepper – 1, diced
- Red bell pepper – 1, diced
- Banana peppers - 4, diced
- Minced fresh thyme - 1 tablespoon

Method
In a 4 quart slow cooker, add everything except peppers and thyme. Cook on high for 3 hours. Stir in peppers and thyme, cook for 4-5 minutes more and serve. You can chill it in the fridge before serving.

Slow cooker rosemary-lemon beets

Colorful, bright beets taste good with lemony flavor.

Serves: 4-5

Ingredients:
- Beets (about 6) – 2 pounds, peeled and cut into wedges
- Fresh lemon juice - 2 tablespoons
- Extra-virgin olive oil - 2 tablespoons
- Agave nectar - 2 tablespoons
- Cider vinegar - 1 tablespoon
- Kosher salt - 3/4 teaspoon
- Freshly ground black pepper - 1/2 teaspoon
- Rosemary sprigs - 2
- Grated lemon rind - 1/2 teaspoon

Method
Combine everything except lemon rind in a 4 quart slow cooker and cook for 8 hours on low. Remove rosemary sprigs and mix lemon rind and serve.

Slow cooker balsamic vinegar collard greens

Serve with mashed potatoes and chili with rice to give a tangy flavor to your meal.

Serves: 4-5

Ingredients:
- Onion - 1 cup, chopped
- Chopped fresh collard greens - 1 (16-ounce) package
- Salt - 1/4 teaspoon
- Garlic – 2, cloves, minced
- Bay leaf - 1
- Fat-free, lower-sodium vegetable broth - 1 (14.5-ounce) can
- Balsamic vinegar - 3 tablespoons
- Agave nectar – 1 teaspoon

Method
In a skillet, stir-fry onion until tender. Add greens and sauté until wilt. In a 4 quart cooker, add everything with the greens mixture except nectar and vinegar. Cook on high for 3 ½ hours. Mix vinegar and nectar and pour over greens before serving.

Risotto with mushroom and barley

It's a healthy vegan version for a hearty party meal.

Serves: 4-5

Ingredients:
- Dried porcini mushrooms - 1 ounce, chopped
- Leek – 1, white and pale green parts only, slit lengthwise
- White mushrooms - 1 pound, sliced
- Pearl barley - 1 1/2 cups, rinsed
- Low-sodium vegetable broth - 4 cups
- Thyme sprigs - 2
- Salt and pepper, to taste
- Fresh flat-leaf parsley - 1/2 cup, finely chopped

Method
Soak the porcinis in water. Reserve half the mushrooms. In a 4 quart cooker, add everything along with the porcinis along with the liquid. Cook for 3 hours on high. Serve risotto with parsley and reserved mushroom toppings.

Black beans in a slow cooker

It's a Mexican staple that can never go wrong as a side dish.

Serves: 4-5

Ingredients:
- Dried black beans - 1 (1-pound) package
- Fat-free, lower-sodium vegetable broth - 3 cups
- Finely chopped onion (about 1 large) - 2 cups
- Chopped chipotle chile, canned in adobo sauce - 1 tablespoon
- Salt - 1 teaspoon
- Garlic - 4 cloves, minced
- Fresh lime juice - 1 tablespoon
- Chopped fresh cilantro - 1/2 cup
- Unsalted pumpkin seed kernels - 1/2 cup

Method
In a saucepan, boil beans for 2-3 minutes and let soak in water for 1 hour. Drain beans. In a slow cooker, add everything with beans except pumpkin seeds and cilantro. Cook on high for 3-4 hours. Mash beans with a potato masher and serve hot with pumpkin seed and cilantro topping.

Crockpot baked potatoes

Extremely simple yet delectable dish to be served on your dining table.

Serves: 4-5

Ingredients:
- Potatoes – 4, well-scrubbed
- Kosher salt, to taste
- Extra virgin olive oil – 1 tablespoon
- Aluminium foil – 4 sheets

Method
On the potatoes, rub salt and olive oil. Wrap each potato lightly in foil sheets. Place in a slow cooker and cook on high for 4-5 hours and on low for 7-8 hours. Serve hot with vegan sour cream topping (optional).

All vegan cabbage rolls

With flavored rice stuffing, this recipe is filling by itself.

Serves: 6

Ingredients:
- Cabbage – 12 leaves
- Cooked white rice – 1 cup
- Egg replacer for 1 egg
- Rice milk - ¼ cup
- Minced onion – ¼ cup
- Salt – 1 ¼ teaspoon
- Ground black pepper – 1 ¼ teaspoon
- Tomato sauce – 1-8 ounces can
- Brown sugar – 1 tablespoon
- Lemon juice – 1 tablespoon
- Worchesteire sauce – 1 tablespoon

Method

In a saucepan, boil cabbage leaves for a few minutes. In a bowl, combine everything except tomato sauce, worchestire sauce, brown sugar and lemon juice. Spoon a little filling in each cabbage leaf and tuck the rolls.

In another bowl, mix the sauces with brown sugar and lemon juice. Place the rolls in a 4 quart slow cooker and pour sauce over them. Cook on low for 7-8 hours.

Main dishes

As the name suggests, main dishes are served at the center of your dining table to complete a meal. Whether it's lunch or dinner time, main dishes are always the focus point of every meal, hence it should be well cooked with all the essential nutrients.

The best thing about main dishes is that they can be accompanied by various other dishes like rice, breads and side dishes. So, let's have a look at some of the vegan slow cooker main dishes that can be prepared using all vegan ingredients, keeping in mind the taste and nutrition for all.

Note: All these main dishes can be made a day before or cooked overnight in a slow cooker, if you want them for lunch.

Spicy, hot southern chickpeas over grits vegan slow cooker

With liquid smoke, this recipe will offer all the flavors of the real version 'shrimp over grits'. It's an easy recipe as well!

Serves: 1-2

Ingredients:
For chickpeas
- Cooked chickpeas – 1-16 ounces can or 1 ½ cups
- Bell pepper – 1 cup, chopped
- Tomatoes – 1-14.5 ounces can or 1 ½ cups
- Water – ½ cup
- Cajun spice blend – 2 teaspoons
- Chipotle powder – ¼-1/2 teaspoons
- Garlic – 2 cloves, minced
- Smoke salt or liquid smoke – few dashes
- Tobacco or any other hot sauce
- Salt and pepper to taste

For grits:

- White or yellow grits – 1/2 cup
- Unsweetened nondairy milk – 1 cup
- Water – 1 cup
- Vegan bouillon cube – 1
- Salt and pepper to taste

Method

Cook grits in a slow cooker by adding all the ingredients together and cooking on low for 7-9 hours. You can prepare grits a day before, if you do not have two slow cookers.

To cook chickpeas, add all the ingredients in a slow cooker except salt and pepper. Let everything cook for about 7-9 hours at low. While serving, add salt and pepper and adjust flavor by adding more chipotle powder, Cajun blend and liquid smoke, if desired. Serve over hot grits and enjoy the meal.

Sloppy black eyes peas

A simple yet filling meal that is packed with flavor that is guaranteed to satisfy even the pickiest eater. Best served warm.

Serves: 2

Ingredients
For cooking
- Black eyed peas – 48g
- Carrots, chopped -1/3 cup
- Millet – 1/6 cup
- Bell peppers, minced – 1 tablespoon
- Garlic, minced- 1 clove
- Cajun seasoning – 1 teaspoon
- Water – 2 cups
- Liquid smoke – ¼ teaspoon

For serving
- 1 cup minced greens
- 2 tbsp tomato paste
- Salt to taste
- Pepper to taste
- 2-3 buns

Method
Add all the cooking ingredients in the slow cooker and cook on low for 7 to 9 hours. Mix in the serving ingredients to the cooked peas. Spread the peas on lightly toasted buns and serve open faced style.

'Meaty' Vegan Chili

This is indeed a great meal option when your entire family is in the mood to spend time together at the dinner table while savoring delicious chili.

Serves: 4-5

Ingredients:
- Dry black beans – 2 cups
- Water – 6 cups
- Garlic – 4 cloves, minced
- Liquid smoke - A few dashes
- Ground Beefless – 1 cup (use Trader Joe's, frozen crumbles)
- Tomato – 1 cup, diced
- Tomato paste – 2 teaspoons
- Chili powder – 1 teaspoons
- Hot pepper of your choice (optional) – 1 teaspoon
- Regular salt or smoked salt – to taste
- Vegan sour cream (optional) – for serving
- Baked sweet potato for serving

Method
Use a 4 quart slow cooker.

If you want to prepare the dish for dinner, you must start cooking a night ahead.
At night, turn the slow cooker on low and add beans, garlic, liquid smoke and water. Let everything cook at low the whole night.

In the morning, open the cooker and add the rest of the ingredients, but not salt. Mix thoroughly and leave to cook for 8-9 hours.

While serving, garnish with sour cream and serve over baked sweet potato. It will taste good on top of quinoa or rice.

Vegan creamy, garlicky scalloped potatoes

A perfect holiday creamy dinner recipe for the whole family to enjoy. Decorate the dish with extra Cheddar to create 'au gratin'.

Serves: 6

Ingredients:
- Organic or regular potatoes – 2 pounds, peeled if regular else use without peeling
- Cashews – 1 cup
- Nutritional yeast – 1 cup
- Garlic – 5 cloves
- Unsweetened almond milk or rice milk (no soy milk) – 1 ½ cup
- Salt – 1-1 ½ teaspoon
- Pepper – a dash

Method
At night, prepare sauce by adding everything except potatoes in a blender. Blend the sauce till creamy and smooth. In a container, store the sauce and keep in the refrigerator. Thinly slice potatoes and keep in a container filled with water, else the potatoes will change color. Store in the fridge.

In the morning, oil your slow cooker and pour 1/3 of creamy sauce in it. Now, arrange 1/2 potatoes in a layer over sauce. Pour more 1/3 sauce over potato layer and place all remaining potato slices over sauce. End with the rest of the cream. Cover the cooker and cook for 6-8 hours on low.

Your creamy potatoes are ready to gulp!

You can do the preparation in the morning also instead of night.

Slow cooker vegan macaroni with creamy butternut squash sauce

Of course, a healthy choice over conventional mac and cheese as here creaminess is added with butternut squash sauce that will not add calories to your meal!

Serves: 5

Ingredients:
Morning:
- Butternut squash – 1 ½ cups, cubed
- Tomatoes – ½ cup, chopped
- Water – 1 ½ cups
- Garlic – 2 cloves, minced
- Fresh thyme – 3 sprigs of 3 inches or dried thyme – 1 ½ teaspoons
- Fresh rosemary – 1 sprig or 2 inches or dried rosemary – ½ teaspoon

Evening:
- Nutritional yeast flakes – ¼ cup
- Rice milk or almond milk – ½-1 cup
- Whole wheat macaroni – 1 ½ cups, uncooked
- Pepper and salt, to taste
-

Make this dish healthier by adding some chopped broccoli and fresh greens.

Method
Use 1 ½-2 quart slow cooker.
In the morning, add all morning ingredients to slow cooker and cook for 7-9 hours on low.

45 minutes before serving, blend all the slow cooker contents in a blender with the milk you are using and nutritional yeast. Again pour the blended mixture into the cooker and stir in macaroni. Turn on high and cook for 20 minutes.

Add more milk, if the consistency of the sauce is too thick. Let it cook for 15 minutes more or till the macaroni is al dante. Sprinkle pepper and salt and serve hot.

Note: Every 10 minutes, keep on checking your pasta in the cooker to avoid sticking.

Eggplant Tapenade

A yummy veggie spread that is packed with flavors and nutrients for a healthy meal. Best served with bruschetta, crackers or crostini.

Serves: 4

Ingredients
- Eggplants, chopped - 3
- Diced tomatoes – 3 cups
- Green olives, pitted and chopped – 1 can
- Garlic, minced – 4 cloves
- Capers – 2 teaspoons
- Balsamic vinegar – 2 teaspoons
- Dried basil – 1 teaspoon
- Salt to taste
- Pepper to taste

Method
Mix the vinegar, basil, salt and pepper and leave aside. Add everything else in the slow cooker and cook for 7 to 9 hours. Before serving, mix in the vinegar dressing.
Serve either chunky or pureed.

Hide & seek veggie pasta sauce

An excellent sauce with the goodness of fresh vegetables that goes deliciously with pasta. Ideal for feeding unaware picky eaters.

Ingredients
- Garlic cloves, minced – 4-6
- Diced tomatoes – 2 cans
- Carrots, chopped – 1 cup
- Bell pepper, chopped - 1
- Tomato paste – 2 tablespoons
- Fresh basil – 2 tablespoons
- Salt to taste
- Pepper to taste

Method
Mix all the vegetables in a bowl, cover and leave overnight in the refrigerator.
Combine all the ingredients except seasoning in the slow cooker and cook all day on low. Season and taste. Puree well and serve poured over cooked pasta. Enjoy.

Slow cooker tempeh stewed with port wine and figs

A complete meal that would certainly please even the toughest critic! Serve it with roasted asparagus and mashed potato to enjoy at the fullest.

Serves: 4

Ingredients:
- Olive oil – 2 tablespoons
- Onion – 1 small, minced
- Garlic – 2 cloves, minced
- Soy tempeh – 1 packet-8 ounces
- Fresh figs – 8, cut each into 6 wedges
- Water – ½ cup
- Port wine – 1 cup
- Balsamic vinegar – 1 tablespoon (you can use 2 tbsps balsamic vinegar if not using port wine. Add extra water to make 1 cup liquid)
- Vegan bouillon – 1 tablespoon
- Fresh thyme – 1 sprig
- Fresh rosemary – 1 sprig
- Salt and pepper, to taste

Method
Sauté onion and garlic at night to save time. Stir fry both the ingredients in a little oil until tender. Store in a container in the fridge. Cut tempeh and figs also the night before and keep in the fridge.

In the morning, take a 4 quart slow cooker and fill it with all the ingredients. Cook for 6-8 hours on low.

Tempeh chili with Vaquero beans

It's a protein packed dish for a healthy meal. Serve it over rice or quinoa for a hearty lunch or dinner.

Serves: 6

Ingredients:
- Olive oil – 2 tablespoons
- Onion – ½ small, minced
- Garlic – 3 cloves, minced
- Soy tempeh – 8 ounces, diced
- Cooked Vaquero beans – 6 cups or Pinto beans – 3 cans, rinsed and drained
- Water – 4 cups
- Tomatoes – 1 can, diced
- Tomato paste – 1 tablespoon
- Chili powder – 1 teaspoon
- Pasilla chile powder – 1 teaspoon
- Oregano – 1 teaspoon
- Paprika – 1 /2 teaspoon
- Chipotle powder – ¼-1/2 teaspoon
- Plain or smoked salt, to taste
- Cashew cream or vegan sour cream, for serving

Method
In a pan, heat olive oil and sauté onion until tender and translucent. Then add garlic and again stir fry for a few minutes. Remove from the pan. With all the other ingredients except sour cream, put onion-garlic in a slow cooker. Turn on the cooker on high and cook for 4-5 hours.

While serving, top it up with a little sour cream and enjoy!

Vegan Slow cooker Cincinnati Chili

It's a great spaghetti topping for a wholesome meal. Enjoy it either in lunch or at dinner or amuse your guests with its amazing flavors!

Note: Prepare the chili a day before if you want to devour it for lunch.

Serves: 2

Ingredients:
For morning
- Dry black beluga lentils – ¾ cup (use any other lentil if you do not want dark color chili)
- Water – 1 ½ cups
- Garlic – 2 cloves, minced
- Bay leaf – 1
- Grounded vegan crumbles – ½ cup (if you want a soy free version, then use cooked quinoa – ½ cup)
- Ground cumin – 1/2 teaspoon
- Ground hot pepper (any) – ¼ teaspoon
- Ground cinnamon – 1/8 teaspoon
- Chili powder – 1 teaspoon
- Cocoa powder – 1 teaspoon
- Ground allspice – 1 pinch

For evening
- Tomatoes – 1 ½ cups, diced
- Fresh ground nutmeg – a dash
- Salt, to taste
- Cooked pasta – 2-3 cups (for serving)

Method
In the morning, add all the morning ingredients in a 1 ½- 2 quart slow cooker and cook on low for 7-9 hours.

Half an hour before serving, open the cooker and add tomatoes, salt and nutmeg. Cook on high until the tomatoes get smashed and mixed with other ingredients.

Serve hot over cooked pasta and top it up with chopped onions or shredded vegan cheese or cooked beans, all optional though.

Grains and beans slow cooker chili

Chili can never go wrong as a main dish. It works well if you are in a mood to have a family get together or are planning for a formal event. Top it over cooked rice or pasta or simply eat with a taco or quesadillas, you'll love it all the time!

Serves: 3-4

Ingredients:
- Assorted dry beans (no kidney beans) – 2 cups
- Water – 6 cups
- Tomato puree or diced tomatoes – 1 can
- Millet – 1/8 cup
- Dry vegan bouillon – 1 tablespoon
- Cumin – 1 teaspoon
- Chili spice mix – 1 teaspoon
- Ancho powder or chipotle – ½ teaspoon
- Smoked paprika – ½ teaspoon
- Salt, to taste

Method
In a 1-1 ½ quart slow cooker, add beans and 4 cups water at night. Cook for 7-9 hours or overnight on low temperature.

In the morning, remove the beans from the cooker and rinse them. Again add beans with all other ingredients and 2 cups water. Add salt before serving. Now let everything cook on low for 7-10 hours.

Crockpot vegan bean chili with steel-cut oats

Chili is for all seasons and this one is a perfect main dish to be served over cooked quinoa or rice.

Serves: 6

Ingredients:
- Water – 6 cups
- Veggie bouillon – 2 cubes
- Steel-cut oats – 1 /2 cup
- Oregano – 1 tablespoon
- Ground cumin – 2 teaspoons
- Chili powder – 1 teaspoon
- Garlic – 3 cloves, minced
- Kidney beans – 1-14.5 ounces can, drained and rinsed
- Black beans - 1-14.5 ounces can, drained and rinsed
- Tomatoes - 1-14.5 ounces can, diced
- Fire-roasted or regular frozen corns – 1 cup
- Liquid smoke, to taste
- ½ lime juice
- Salt and pepper, to taste

Method
In a 1-1 ½ quart slow cooker, add everything except lime juice and salt & pepper.

Cook for 7-10 hours on low heat. Before serving, add salt & pepper and squeeze ½ lime over chili.

Vegan Pumpkin lasagna

This recipe has been tweaked for calorie conscious people. It's a variation of heavy fate loaded conventional lasagna. Serve it with balsamic vinaigrette spinach salad and you are all set for a hearty dinner meal.

Note: Cook it on high for 1 1/2 – 2 hours if you do not want your lasagna to turn mushy after a long day in a slow cooker.

Serves: 3-4

Ingredients:
For pumpkin tofu 'Ricotta'
- Tofu – 1 container
- Cooked pumpkin – 1-15 oz. can or equivalent fresh cooked pumpkin
- Nutritional yeast – ¼ cup
- Italian seasoning – 1 tablespoon
- Onion powder – 1 teaspoon
- Garlic – 2 cloves, crushed
- Olive oil – 1 tablespoon
- Sun-dried tomatoes – 3, soaked-in water and minced
- Salt and pepper to taste
-

Prepare "Ricotta" in a blender, add tomatoes and olive oil and blend to make a smooth paste. Then add all other ingredients and process to make a creamy sauce.
Store in the refrigerator till morning.

For Lasagna
- Pumpkin Tofu "Ricotta" – 1 batch (as above)
- Whole wheat lasagna – ¾ packet
- Organic marinara sauce – 1 jar (homemade can also be used)
- Cooked white beans – 1-16 oz can

Method

1/2-2 hours prior to serving, brush a little olive oil at the bottom of 1-1 ½ quart crockpot to avoid sticking. Cut the lasagna sides to make it fit comfortably in crockpot. Now start layering the lasagna. Spread marinara sauce at the crockpot bottom and put a lasagna layer and top with "Ricotta". Repeat this step until you reach the last layer of lasagna and top that end layer with marinara sauce.

In a slow cooker, cook for 1 ½-2 hours on high.

Slow cooker chickpea-pumpkin chili

With an intense flavor of cilantro, healthy pumpkin and chickpeas, this dish will make a great holiday meal!

Serves: 10

Ingredients:
- Onion - 1 diced
- Garlic – 2 cloves, minced
- Green bell pepper - 1/2, diced
- Salt - 1/2 to 1 teaspoon
- Olive oil - 1 tablespoon
- Frozen or fresh corn - 1 cup
- Diced tomatoes - 1 can - 28 ounces
- Pumpkin puree - 1 can (15 ounces)
- Chickpeas - 1 can (15 ounces), drained and rinsed
- Black beans - 1 can (15 ounces), drained and rinsed
- Chili powder - 1 to 3 teaspoons
- Cumin - 2 teaspoons
- Vegetable broth - 1 cup
- 1 lime juice and zest
- Black pepper to taste
- Cilantro - 1/4 to 1/2 cup, minced, for garnish

Method
In a pan, stir fry onion and garlic until tender. Take a 4 quart slow cooker and fill it with all the ingredients along with onion-garlic but keep cilantro for garnish. Turn cooker on low and cook everything for 7-9 hours.

Serve chili with cilantro on top and cooked rice on side.

Vegan Barley Risotto with root veggies

With whole grain barley and inexpensive yet delicious root veggies like rutabaga and turnip, this slow cooker dish will end up making you go wow! It's oil-free too, so enjoy it without guilt.

Serves: 2-3

Ingredients:
Morning ingredients
- Water – 2 cups
- Barley – ½ cup
- Carrots – ½ cup, diced
- Turnips or rutabagas – ½ cup, diced and peeled
- Sweet potatoes – ½ cup, diced or (70 g) winter squash
- Garlic - 2 cloves, minced
- Dried oregano - ½ teaspoon
- Dried sage - ½ teaspoon

Evening ingredients:
- Greens (such as kale, collards, turnips, etc.) – 1 cup, minced
- Lemon zest – ¼ teaspoon
- Salt and pepper, to taste

Method
In the morning, take a 1-1 ½ quart slow cooker and fill it with all the ingredients. Cook for 7-9 hours at low.

Half an hour prior to serving, add greens and lemon zest to slow cooker. Sprinkle salt and pepper while serving. Add more sage and oregano to adjust flavor while serving.

Eat it up with a crispy garlic bread.

Indian-style stew with mixed lentils

Those who like subtle flavors of Indian spices can enjoy this wonderful stew either at lunch or for dinner. Top it up over fragrant white rice to fill your appetite.

Serves: 2-3

Ingredients:
- Water – 4 cups
- Cherry tomatoes - 1/2 cup, cut in quarters
- Potato - 1/2 cup, chopped
- Red lentils - 1/2 cup
- Brown lentils - 1/2 cup
- Yellow split peas – ½ cup
- Black cardamom -2 pods
- Turmeric powder - 1 teaspoon
- Cumin seed - 1/2 teaspoon
- Mustard seeds - 1/2 teaspoon
- Ground coriander - 1/2 teaspoon
- Fenugreek seeds - 1/2 teaspoon
- Ground cinnamon - 1/4 teaspoon
- Chili flakes - 1/4 to 1/2 teaspoon, to taste
- Salt, to taste

Method
Take a 2 quart cooker; but if you have 1 ½ quarts cooker, then reduce 2 cups of water and ¼ cup of lentils.

Put everything in the cooker and cook for 7-9 hours at low temperature. While serving, adjust the salt and flavor by adding more ground spices.

Slow cooker mushroom tempeh stroganoff

It's a simple and amazingly great stroganoff with delicious taste. Even with less ingredients, this dish comes with a good broth that is made due to mushrooms. Cook it up in a slow cooker to let the flavors penetrate thoroughly.

Serves: 2-3

Ingredients:
- Tempeh - 1 package (8 ounces)
- Mushrooms - 2 cups- 5 ounces, chopped small
- Garlic - 2 cloves, minced
- Water - 1 to 2 cups, use more if you will cook longer than 8 hours
- Vegan Bouillon – 1 teaspoon
- Paprika - 1/2 teaspoon
- Vegan sour cream - 1/3 cup (cashew cream or unsweetened non-dairy milk)
- A pinch dill, optional
- Salt and pepper, to taste

Cooked pasta, for serving

Method
At night: Steam tempeh for around 10 minutes to remove its bitterness. Store with chopped mushrooms in the fridge.

In the morning: Take a 3 quart slow cooker, but if you have 2 or less quarts cooker, reduce the quantity of the ingredients accordingly.

Put tempeh, mushrooms, water, bouillon and garlic in the cooker and cook on low for 7-10 hours.

White serving add sour cream, salt and pepper, paprika and dill.

Vegan slow cooker red beans with rice

This gluten-free and soy-free recipe is incredibly delectable and quantity can be adjusted as per your family size!

Serves: 2-3

Ingredients:
- Dry red beans – 1 cup
- Water – 3 cups
- Garlic - 2 cloves, minced
- Bay leaves - 2
- Cajun seasoning (salt-free) - 1 teaspoon
- Smoked salt or liquid smoke – few drops
- Tabasco sauce, optional (to taste or serve on the side)
- Salt, to taste

Cooked rice for serving

Method
Take a 1-1 ½ quart slow cooker and fill it up with water, dry beans, bay leaves and garlic. Cook on low for the whole night.

In the morning, add to the cooker: liquid smoke, Cajun seasoning, and Tabasco sauce, if using. You can add more water according to the time you want it to cook for the day.

Before serving, add salt and adjust seasoning as per your taste.

Serve on top of cooked rice and vegan sausages or grilled tofu (optional).

Slow cooker black beans with Mexican quinoa

It's an oil-free dish with lots of health added to make it a wholesome meal.

Serves: 4

Ingredients:
- Bell pepper - 1 1/2 cup, chopped
- Garlic - 3 cloves, minced
- Water - 2 1/2 cups
- Tomatoes - 1 1/2 cups, diced (or a 14.5 ounce can – do not drain)
- Cooked black beans - 1 1/2 cups or 1 can (15 oz), rinsed and drained
- Vegetable bouillon - 1 cube
- Chili powder- 1 to 2 teaspoons
- Cumin - 1/2 teaspoon
- Quinoa - 3/4 cup, rinsed well
- Salt and pepper to taste

Method

At night: Rinse the beans, if using canned and prepare the veggies. Keep everything in the refrigerator.

In the morning: Oil a 4 quart slow cooker and add everything except salt & pepper and quinoa. Cook on low temperature for 6-8 hours.

1-2 hours prior to serving, add quinoa to cooker. Turn on high and cook until quinoa starts to wilt. Adjust seasonings with chili powder and cumin. Serve hot.

Crock pot vegetables with spaghetti

This is an affordable meal with some 'great' flavors. You can make it gluten-free by using brown spaghetti, but any pasta will do!

Serves: 5

Ingredients:
- Pasta - 1/2 package
- Water - 2 cups
- Green pepper – 1, chopped
- Onion – ½, diced
- Garlic - 2 cloves, minced
- Red pepper – 1, chopped
- Mushrooms - 5-7 , sliced
- Fresh tomatoes - 3 cups, diced or 1-28oz can diced tomatoes
- Fresh basil – 2 tablespoons, chopped
- Fresh parsley – 2 tablespoons, chopped
- Salt to taste

Method:
In a 2 quarts slow cooker, add everything except pasts, parsley and basil. Cook on low for 30 minutes.

Then cook on high for 1 1 /2 hours until onion becomes tender. Just 20 minutes prior to cooking end time, add pasta. 5 minutes before the spaghetti is cooked, stir in basil and parsley.

Serve hot for lunch or dinner with crispy garlic bread.

Slow cooker tempeh-quinoa jambalaya

Straight and simple main dish for a hearty meal. You can add variation by putting fast-cooking veggies like peas, greens, broccoli etc. to turn it into a stew.

Serves: 4

Ingredients:
- Bell pepper - 1 1/2 cup, chopped
- Garlic - 3 cloves, minced
- Tempeh - 8 ounces, cut into bite-sized pieces
- Water - 3 cups
- Tomatoes - 1 1/2 cups, diced (or 14.5 ounce can – do not drain)
- Non-chicken bouillon - 1 tablespoon
- Cajun seasoning - 1 to 2 teaspoons
- Liquid smoke or smoked paprika - 1/4 to 1/2
- Quinoa - 3/4 cup, rinsed well
- Salt and pepper to taste, if needed
- Tabasco or hot pepper, optional

Method

At night: Cut all the vegetables and steam tempeh for 10 minutes, if desired. Keep everything in the fridge.

In the morning: Take a 3 quart slow cooker and add all the ingredients except quinoa, Tabasco and salt & pepper.

1-2 hours prior to serving, add quinoa and cook till the time quinoa wilts. Add hot pepper or Tabasco with salt and pepper.

Slow cooker cornbread and beans casserole

This is a simple and truly sumptuous vegan dish that will make your stomach growl! Have it on a rainy afternoon to feel cozy.

Serves: 6

- Green or red bell pepper – 1, chopped
- White or sweet onion – 1, chopped
- Garlic - 3 cloves, minced
- Red kidney beans, Pinto beans, Black beans - 1 can (15oz) for each, drained and rinsed
- Tomato sauce – 10oz
- Diced tomatoes w/ chilies - 15 oz can
- Cream corn - 1 can, halved
- Chili powder - 2 teaspoons
- Pepper - 1 teaspoon
- Salt - 2 teaspoon
- Hot sauce - 1 teaspoon
- Yellow corn meal, AP flour - 1/2 cup each
- Baking powder - 1 1/4 teaspoon
- Sugar, salt – 1 tablespoon each
- Non-dairy milk - 3/4 cup
- 1 egg replacer mix of choice (chia seeds and banana)
- Vegetable oil - 1 1/2 tablespoon

Method

Take a 4 quart slow cooker and spray it with a little oil. In a pan, add onion, garlic and beans and water stir-fry until tender. Put this mixture in the slow cooker along with tomatoes, tomato sauce, beans, hot sauce, spices and ½ can-creamed corn. Mix well, cover the cooker and cook for 1 hour on high.

In a mixing bowl, add AP flour, cornmeal, baking powder, salt, sugar, egg replacer, non-dairy milk and oil. Add the remaining ½ can-creamed corn. Mix well.

In the cooker, spread this paste over the beans. Make it smooth. Cover the cooker again and cook for 90 minutes on high. Cut a piece of cornbread to check if it's done.

Easy Slow cooker lentil chilli

This is an easy main dish that goes well with both brown rice and quinoa. Moreover, it's not too spicy, so you can enjoy it without getting 'fire' on your tongue!

Serves 12

Ingredients:
- Olive oil - 1 tablespoon
- Onions - 2 medium, chopped
- Garlic - 6-8 cloves, minced
- Carrots - 2, chopped
- Celery – 1 stalk, chopped
- Chili powder, cumin powder - 2 tablespoons each
- Coriander powder, dried oregano, dry mustard - 1 teaspoon each
- Crushed tomatoes - One 28-ounce box
- Salt to taste
- Dry lentils - One 16-ounce package, picked through for stones, rinsed and drained
- Vegetable broth - 6-7 cups

Method
In a pan, heat oil and sauté onion, garlic, celery and carrot until all turn tender and onion becomes brown. Now add tomatoes and all spices. Now take a 4 quart slow cooker and add dry lentils along with spice-tomato mix. Add broth and cook on high for 4-5 hours. Add more water or broth to adjust the consistency.

Crock pot mushroom-meatless sausage Ragu

It's a nice dish for dinner parties with 'vegan' effect. The best thing about this dish is it freezes well! So you can devour the leftovers later on as well.

Serves 4

Ingredients:
- Olive oil – 1 teaspoon
- Onion - 1, minced
- Garlic - 3 cloves, minced
- Gimme Lean Sausage - 1 package
- Organic crushed tomatoes - 2- 28 oz. cans
- Crimini mushrooms, chopped - 16 oz.
- Portabella mushrooms - 2 large, chopped
- Fresh basil – 2 tablespoons
- Fresh ground pepper to taste
- Balsamic vinegar – 1 tablespoon
- Red wine or port wine - 2 – 3 tablespoons

Method
At night: In a pan, heat olive oil and stir-fry onion till tender. Remove onion from pan and add Lean sausages and stir-fry. Chop them into pieces to make a crumble. Now store everything in the fridge.

In the morning: Take a 3 quart slow cooker and add everything except port wine. Cook on low temperature for 7-10 hours. Add port wine just 10-15 minutes before serving. Adjust seasonings while serving.

Desserts to end your feast

After a sumptuous meal, a dessert is the best way to give your feast a sweet end. Usually, desserts are loaded with heavy cream and other calorific ingredients, but in this vegan recipe book, we are offering you a repertoire of cream-free, fat-free dessert recipes for your sweet tooth.

Crockpot carrot cake with yummy applesauce

With less fat and delicious applesauce, this cake is a perfect sweet dish.

Serves: 3-4

Ingredients:
- Applesauce – ¼ cup
- Vanilla – 1 teaspoon
- Vegan margarine – ½ cup, softened
- Salt – 1 teaspoon
- Baking powder – 1 ½ teaspoon
- Cinnamon – 2 teaspoons
- Sugar – 1 cup
- Flour – 1 ¼ cups
- Soy milk – ¼ cup
- Carrots – 1 cup grated

Method
In a bowl, mix everything to form a cake batter. Pour the batter in a 4 quart slow cooker and cook for 2 ½ hours on high. Insert a knife to check. If it comes out clean, your cake is ready. Sprinkle some chopped walnuts on the cake before serving.

Guilt-free chocolate applesauce vegan cake

It's a completely fat-free moist cake to enjoy after a hearty meal.

Serves: 3-4

Ingredients:
- Flour – 2 cups
- Sugar – 1 cup
- Cornstarch – 1 tablespoon
- Baking soda – 2 teaspoons
- Salt – ¼ teaspoon
- Cocoa – 1/3 cup
- Applesauce – 1 ½ cups

Method
In a bowl, mix all the ingredients and pour the batter in a 4 quart slow cooker. Cook on high for 2 ½ hours until the knife comes out clean. Frost with icing sugar, if desired.

Quick slow cooker soda cake

You won't believe it's so easy to make. Surprise your guests with this 'no-preparation' dessert.

Serves: 3-4

Ingredients:
- Vegan cake mix (any flavor you like) – 1 package
- Cola or sprite – 10 oz. from 12 oz. can

Method
Stir cola in a cake mix thoroughly. Pour the batter in a 3 quart slow cooker and cook for 2 ½ hours on high setting. Check the cake with a knife. If it comes out clean, your cake is ready.

Crockpot key lime pie

With just 5 ingredients, you can make this delicious vegan pie. Try it!

Serves: 3-4

Ingredients:
- Non-dairy cream cheese – 2 can-8 ounces each
- Sugar – 1 cup
- Vanilla – 1 teaspoon
- Lime juice – ¼ cup
- Cornstarch – 2 tablespoons
- Pre-made pie crust – 1

Method
Blend pie topping ingredients in a blender until smooth. In a 4 quart slow cooker, spread a foil sheet at the bottom. Grease the sheet and place a pie crust over it. Pour the lime batter over the crust and cook on high heat for 2 hours. Let the pie completely cook in the crock of the cooker. Remove the foil sheet and chill the pie before serving.

Fat-free sweet potato pie

Its traditional pie with no-fat, truly vegan and calorie-free. What else you'd want from a dessert?

Serves: 4-5

Ingredients:
- Vegan double crust pie – 9 inches
- Water – 1 cup
- Salt – ½ teaspoon
- Sweet potatoes – 3 medium, cubed
- White sugar – ½ cup
- Brown sugar – 1/3 cup
- Lemon juice – 2 tablespoons
- All-purpose flour – 2 tablespoons
- Pumpkin pie spice – 1 tablespoon
- Vegan margarine – 1 tablespoon

Method
In a saucepan, boil sweet potato in water with salt until tender. Drain and mix sweet potato with other ingredients to coat all the pieces well.

Line a 4 quart slow cooker with a foil sheet at the bottom. Spray sheet with oil and place a pie sheet at the bottom. Pour the sweet potato mix on the pie sheet. Drop margarine over the mix. Now cover with another pie sheet. Cook on high for 3 hours or until the pie is done. Let it cool and then refrigerate.

Crock pot chocolate flavored peanut butter cake

Vegan version of classic cake is the ultimate show stopper.

Serves: 4-5

Ingredients:
- Flour – 1 cup
- Sugar – ½ cup+3/4 cup
- Cocoa powder – 3 tablespoons + ¼ cup
- Baking powder – 1 ½ teaspoons
- Soy milk – ½ cup
- Vegan margarine – 2 tablespoons, melted
- Vanilla – 1 teaspoon
- Boiling water – 2 cups
- Peanut butter – ½ cup

Method

In a large bowl, combine flour, ½ cup sugar, baking powder and ¾ cup cocoa powder. Whisk well with margarine, soy milk and vanilla. In a greased 4 quart slow cooker, pour the batter.

In another bowl, mix remaining cocoa powder and sugar. Add boiling water and peanut butter. Whisk well. Pour it over the flour batter in a slow cooker. Cook for 2 ½ hours on high. Enjoy your vegan cake.

Vegan poppy seed lemony cake

It's a fluffy cake with fresh lemon flavor to make your guests go wow!

Serves: 3-4

Ingredients:
- Lemons - 3
- Nondairy creamer - 1 1/4 cups
- Flour - 2 2/3 cups
- Poppy seeds – 2 tablespoons
- Baking soda – 3 teaspoons
- Salt – ¾ teaspoons
- Vegan margarine - 3/4 cup, softened
- Sugar - 2 cups
- Egg replacer for 3 eggs
- Vanilla - 1/2 tsp

Method
Using an electric beater, beat all the ingredients well on high speed until smooth and fluffy. Lightly grease a 4 quart slow cooker and pour the batter in it. Cook on high temperature for 2 ½ hours. Your cake is ready.

Crockpot cherry pie dump cake

This simple cake using just 3 ingredients is a must dessert in a lavish meal.

Serves: 3-4

Ingredients:
- Cherry pie filling – 1 can of 20 ounce
- Vegan yellow cake mix – 1 box
- Vegan margarine – ½ cup, melted

Method

In a slow cooker, place the cherry pie filling. Combine cake mix and margarine in a bowl and pour it over the pie. Cook on high for 3 hours and check with a knife. If it comes out clean, your pie cake is ready!

Slow cooker apple torte

With the goodness of apple, this torte recipe is a sure shot hit in every party.

Serves: 3-4

- Vegan margarine - 1/2 cup, softened
- Sugar - 1 cup + 2 tbsp
- Egg replacer for 4 eggs
- Flour - 1 1/2 cups
- Baking powder - 1/2 tsp
- Soy milk - 2 tbsp
- Apples - 4 or 5, sliced thin
- Cinnamon - 1/2 tsp
- Sliced almonds - 1/2 cup (optional)
- Powdered sugar - 1 tbsp

Method

With a powerful blender, whisk all the ingredients until fluffy and smooth. In a lightly greased 4 quart slow cooker, pour the batter. Place sliced apple on top of batter. Cook for 3 hours on high setting and check with knife. Clean knife means torte is ready.

Vegan low-calorie rice pudding

For a satisfying dessert, go for this sugarless pudding.

Serves :2-3

Ingredients:
- Almond milk – 4 cups
- Rice – ½ cup
- Brown sugar – ¼ cup
- Maple syrup – 2 tablespoons
- Cinnamon and cardamom powder – ¼ teaspoon each
- Raisins – ¼ cup

Method
In a 4 quart slow cooker, combine all the ingredients except raisins and cook on low for 4-6 hours until rice are tender. Serve warm or chilled with raisin toppings.

Diet bread pudding in a slow cooker

It's a traditional dessert, but amazingly different from fatty version. Try it and you'll love it.

Serves: 3-4

Ingredients:
- Bread – 4 cups
- Soy milk – 3 cups
- Sugar – ¾ tablespoon
- Vanilla – 1 tablespoon
- Cinnamon powder – 1 teaspoon
- Raisins – 1 cup
- Almonds – ½ cup chopped

Method
Lightly grease a 4 quart cooker and place bread at the bottom. Combine everything else in a bowl and pour over the bread. Toss the bread lightly to mix with batter.

Cook on high for 20-30 minutes and your pudding is done.

Blueberry Lemon cake

A delicious dessert that is completely soy-gluten-fat free that takes you on a guilt-free indulgence of awesome taste. The cake is best enjoyed with a cup of tea or coffee.

Serves: 4

Ingredients
- Whole wheat pastry flour (gluten-free) – 60 gram
- Non-dairy unsweetened milk – 80 ml
- Blueberries – ¼ cup
- Ground flaxseed (mixed in 2 tsp warm water) – 1 teaspoon
- Lemon zest – ½ teaspoon
- Vanilla extract- ¼ teaspoon
- Lemon extract – ¼ teaspoon
- Olive oil (or applesauce) – 1 teaspoon
- Baking powder – ¼ teaspoon
- Sweetener of your choice – 1 teaspoon

Method
Line a baking tin with parchment paper. Mix the dry and wet ingredients in two separate bowls. Combine both the mixtures and pour into the tin. Spread evenly and cook on high for 60 to 80 minutes or until the center of the cake is solid.

Cool. Cut into slices or wedges and serve.

Free Ebook Offer

The Ultimate Guide To Vitamins

I'm very excited to be able to make this offer to you. This is a wonderful 10k word ebook that has been made available to you through my publisher, Valerian Press. As a health conscious person you should be well aware of the uses and health benefits of each of the vitamins that should make up our diet. This book gives you an easy to understand, scientific explanation of the vitamin followed by the recommended daily dosage. It then highlights all the important health benefits of each vitamin. A list of the best sources of each vitamin is provided and you are also given some actionable next steps for each vitamin to make sure you are utilizing the information!

As well as receiving the free ebooks you will also be sent a weekly stream of free ebooks, again from my publishing company Valerian Press. You can expect to receive at least a new, free ebook each and every week. Sometimes you might receive a massive 10 free books in a week!

All you need to do is simply click here

Alternatively you can type this link into your browser: http://bit.ly/18hmup4

Free Preview Of "The Vegan Diet For Beginners"

I have included a preview chapter of my book, The Vegan Diet For Beginners. This book includes all the background information on the vegan diet as well as plenty of tips to help make the transistion! It contains 8 weeks of diet plans and a further 50 delicious vegan recipes.

To get it, simply click here or type this link into your web-browser:

http://amzn.to/1FAOpJh

15 helpful tips for jumping into the Vegan Diet

1. Have an open mind. Try not to focus on the stigma associated with "hippies" and "vegan" diets. Think of it more as a whole food, plant based diet. A good attitude will help you go a long way. Friends that you know will mock you perhaps don't need to know about your choice until they have personally noticed improvements in your appearance and energy. This is a tough decision and while it can seem strong to stand in the face of opposition, too much opposition will weigh you down. So stick with those who support you at first.

2. If you are cooking at home, allow additional time for the preparations. For many people, designing meals that revolve around whole foods and plants is new, and it can take a lot of extra preparation at the start. Expect to spend a bit longer cooking before you start and it will not present itself as a frustration. Be assured that as you gain experience with the new style of cooking and preparing food your speed will increase!

3. Look over your pantry. Make sure you stock it with whole grains and beans, dried rice, lentils, etc... You want to either prepare and store, or buy vegan friendly sauces and dips too. If you go to cook a vegan meal and all you see in

the cupboards are meat based condiments and processed foods, it will be a challenge.

4. Start making vegan versions of meals you already love. You will hardly notice the difference, but your body certainly will. I have provided loads of examples later in the book and there is a huge amount of recipes online.

5. Read as many recipe books and recipes as you can, including all of those listed in the back of this book. The more you know, the more excited you will be about exploring new options. You will be stunned at how many exciting versions of meals you love can be made vegan friendly!

6. Try dairy alternatives, but start with one to two alternatives per week. This will allow your body to better adjust.

7. Sample vegan foods in places that serve vegan friendly options. There are many new restaurants that focus on this type of diet, and you can locate some in your area. Most restaurants will provide vegan friendly options if you just ask.

8. Avoid convenience foods. You will not enjoy vegan frozen pizzas or frozen burger patties. Seriously, you will be much better off if you just make them at home. The extra work is well worth it. If you hesitate at all, think back to the last time you ate a delicious frozen meal. It probably never happened. Now increase the bad taste and sick feeling you had all night after by a factor of five and that is what your frozen vegan foods will be.

9. Stick to the produce section. You will find that you can load up now on vegetables that you may never have tried before. If you see something in the produce area that you have never even heard of, buy it and look up some recipes for it. See how you like it. You might be surprised! Try everything once, you never know when you are going to find your new favorite food. And remember, that in most stores, the layout for healthy eating is to stick to the perimeter where the produce is. Things in the middle are frozen foods and processed foods. Avoid those.

10. Do not try and "explain" yourself to others. Stick to your guns and let their question serve as a starting point for a

serious conversation about how you agree with the science today, or you have always wanted to try it and you will get more respect from the person on the other end. You might even influence their thinking!

11. When you are heading on a road trip or going to the office, pack your own food. You will feel so much better if you have a bag of carrot sticks and red pepper slices with a package of homemade hummus for your snack or a good salad. Make your own trail mix and see how much easier it will be should you wind up in an unfamiliar location and starving. And on that note...

12. If you *are* in an unfamiliar location and you absolutely need food, do not starve yourself just because you cannot find a vegan option. The moment your eating habits stop being fun, they will seem more like a fad diet and you won't want to continue. Just look for the healthiest option you can find and move on.

13. If you slip up here or there, don't worry. Everyone does. And just because you accidentally had fish sauce or ate something prepared with egg does not mean you are a failure or that you are responsible for the harm and death of millions of animals. No one will kick you out of their group or stop interacting with you because of it. This is a lifestyle change and that takes time.

14. Stay strong! This type of change can be really difficult at first. You might struggle to find vegan friendly foods at home or out and you might think that it is just easier to cave. But don't give in, the health benefits are so worth it!

15. Finally, don't judge other people just because you disagree with their eating habits. If you don't want to be judged by them, don't judge back.

Shopping Guide

When you shop as a vegan you should make sure that you fill your pantry first with the dry staple foods. This includes the following:

- Dried or canned lentils, chickpeas, kidney beans, and pinto beans

- Whole grain pasta and noodles
- Silken tofu
- Unsweetened coconut milk or coconut milk
- Canned tomato and vegetable products
- Soy sauce, vegan mustard, chutney, and other condiments
- Dried fruits
- Thickeners
- Egg replacement powder
- Vegetable broth
- Vinegars
- Grains such as millet, barley, rolled oats, couscous, rice
- Whole grain flour
- Whole grain bread and tortillas
- Nuts and seeds
- Oils
- Almond butter
- Lemons and limes
- Fresh ginger
- Garlic

Then you need to buy your produce. This is really based on whatever you decide to cook, and whatever items you need. With produce you will have to make more regular trips to get fresh products, as not all of them will save well. But that is well worth the health benefits you will receive.

Growing At Home

One of the easiest ways to transition into this diet is to start a small garden at home, even if you just have a standing greenhouse on a balcony or on a window sill. Growing a garden at home can save you so much time and money over the long run and will make it easier to maintain this healthier diet. Instead of having to hope that you can find the ingredients you need, free from any chemicals or additives, you can rest assured knowing that they are right there in your garden. You can stick to a whole food, plant based diet and enjoy the multiple benefits that are associated with tending a small garden. All you'll need to do is stock up on whole grains and then pick daily from your garden the items you want to include for your meals.

A full guide to growing foods at home would warrant another full book so I will simply highlight some of the best foods to grow at home and encourage you to do a little research! It's truly worth it, one of my favorite parts of the day is picking from my home mini-farm and consuming the foods right away, as fresh as can be.

Here is a list of the ten fruits, vegetables and herbs that I believe are the easiest to grow at home: Sweetcorn, peppers, tomatoes, zucchini, cilantro, basil and mint, all kinds of berries, kale and peas.

Eating Out

As a vegan, eating out can be difficult. If you know you are taking a trip soon, you can use resources such as PETA's website or the Happy Cow website to find vegetarian and vegan restaurant chains near your location. Of course, your office might be sending you to a place where fried mayonnaise balls are the norm, in which case, you might want to pack your own food or find accommodations with a small kitchenette and prepare food yourself.

If you are invited to dinner somewhere, plan ahead by looking up the menu. You may not be able to find vegan friendly items, but you might be able to find a vegetarian option. Alternatively, ask if you can modify your foods ahead of time, such as removing chicken from a chicken stir fry. Do not be afraid to call the restaurant if there is no website or menu posted and ask them ahead of time if they can accommodate vegan diets. If you let them know ahead of time, they might be able to speak with the chef before you and your group arrives. You can even ask if they have a vegetarian menu. Some higher end restaurants have a secret vegetarian menu that they only pull out upon request. You might have to lend a hand to the chef by asking them to make a vegetarian dish a vegan one through replacing butter with oil or removing the cheese. If nothing else, you can ask them for a handful of side dishes, like steamed broccoli, beans, and rice, and use that to create your full meal.

If you will be severely limited when going out, say your friends are taking you to a Brazilian restaurant where the dinner is meat with sides of endless meat; you can eat before you go so that you don't need much when you go out. Alternatively, you can search for ethnic restaurants, as these are most likely to have easily modified vegetarian options.

The key here is planning ahead!

Making Small Changes

One of the best ways to remain healthy mentally, physically, and emotionally is changing your diet. Do not rapidly change your diet because this can cause diarrhea, gas, or abdominal cramps. However, gradual changes and higher incorporations of fiber can help your system reduce the bacteria in your colon. There are certain foods which can be integrated into your diet to help increase fiber intake and reduce problems within your colon and digestive system. Whole grains, fruits, and vegetables high in fiber can help to offset these drastic changes to your body.

Cravings

As you make the change toward the vegan diet, your body might start to crave things. When you start to make dietary changes, you may need to test the waters a bit with different recipes and you might have to experience a learning curve before you can find meals and recipes that give you all of the nutrients you need and help to keep you energized. You may experience cravings at first which indicate that your body is not consuming enough. But you might also get a craving for another reason.

Your body will naturally crave things when it requires a particular nutrient and being able to recognize those cravings can enable you to incorporate whatever nutrient is missing into your next meal.

When you feel a deep crave for chocolate it means your body needs magnesium. When this happens try to incorporate the following into your next meal:

- Nuts
- Seeds
- Fruit
- Legumes

If your body is craving sweets or sugary foods it needs things such as Chromium, Phosphorous, Sulphur, Carbon, or Tryptophan. When this happens it is best to incorporate:

- Fresh fruit
- Broccoli
- Raisins
- Sweet potatoes
- Grapes
- Spinach
- Nuts

When you feel a deep crave for bread or pasta your body needs nitrogen. When this happens try to incorporate the following into your next meal:

- Beans
- Nuts

When you feel a deep crave for oily foods or fatty foods your body needs calcium. When this happens try to incorporate the following into your next meal

- Green leafy vegetables
- Broccoli

If you are overeating your body may need silicon or tyrosine so you should eat:

- Spinach
- Nuts
- Seeds
- Fruit
- Vegetables

- Raisins

To get it, simply type this link into your web-browser:

http://amzn.to/1FAOpJh

About the Author

Hello! I'm Jessica Brooks, relatively new to the world of authorship but a veteran of the health and diet industry. If you have read any of my books, I would like to thank you from the bottom of my heart. I truly hope they have helped answer your questions and injected some inspiration into your life. Thanks to my wonderful upbringing I have been a vegetarian since infancy, making to jump to veganism nearly 20 years ago. I'm passionate about helping people improve their health! Over the coming months I am hoping to write a couple more books that will help people learn, start and succeed with certain diets.

In my spare time I am an avid reader of fantasy fiction (George Martin, you demon!). You can often find me lounging in my hammock with my latest book well into the evening. Outside of reading, I love all things physical. From hiking to sailing, swimming to skiing I'm a fan of it all! I try to practice Yoga a couple of times a week, I really recommend everyone gives it a try. You will just feel amazing after a good session!

You can find a facebook page I help manage here:

https://www.facebook.com/CleanFoodDiet

I would like to thank my publishers Valerian Press for giving me the opportunity to create this book.

Valerian Press

At Valerian Press we have three key beliefs.

Providing outstanding value: We believe in enriching all of our customers' lives, doing everything we can to ensure the best experience.

Championing new talent: We believe in showcasing the worlds emerging talent by giving them the platform to grow.

Simplicity and efficiency: We understand how valuable your time is. Our products are stream-lined and consist only of what you want. You will find no fluff with us.

We hope you have enjoyed reading Jessica's Vegan Slow Cooker Cookbook.

We would love to offer you a regular supply of our free and discounted books. We cover a huge range of non-fiction genres; diet and cookbooks, health and fitness, alternative and holistic medicine, spirituality and plenty more. All you need to do is type this link into your web browser: http://bit.ly/18hmup4

Printed in Great Britain
by Amazon.co.uk, Ltd.,
Marston Gate.